The Mentoring Guide

The Mentoring Guide

Helping Mentors & Mentees Succeed

Vineet Chopra, MD, MSc
Valerie M. Vaughn, MD, MSc
Sanjay Saint, MD, MPH

Published in the United States of America by
Michigan Publishing
Manufactured in the United States of America

ISBN 978-1-60785-539-2 (paper)
ISBN 978-1-60785-540-8 (e-book)

TABLE OF CONTENTS

FOREWORD

Although I run mentoring programs at the University of Chicago and have mentored many trainees, I must confess a horrible secret. I loathe the question "Will you be my mentor?" It is not that I do not like to mentor. In fact, I love being a mentor. However, I am engulfed in expectations and worry when faced with this question. If I say yes, I fear I may overcommit and underdeliver, as an example of one of the various forms of "mentor malpractice" that are outlined in this guide. If I say no, I feel like I have abandoned someone in their time of greatest need. To be honest, I have not had a good structured approach for how to really answer this question. Thanks to *The Mentoring Guide* by Chopra, Vaughn, and Saint, I now have a framework for how to deal with this quandary. In fact, agreeing to mentor everyone would be mentor malpractice. I can say no but offer to serve in a different role: as a coach, sponsor, or connector. This simple "aha" has changed my professional life. I now routinely say, "I cannot mentor you but I can coach you," or "I am not sure I am the best mentor for you, but let me connect you to someone who can be a mentor for you."

Indeed, one of the most common things I do is to coach medical trainees on how to find mentors. Initially, everyone is "looking for the one." They bemoan that they can't find the "one" because this person is busy, that person is available but is not in their field, or this other person is too junior to mentor. Unfortunately, the concept of "monogamous mentoring" or a "mentor-mentee dyad" is especially prevalent in healthcare and even more so in health services research, where our trainees list their one main mentor as the advisor on their first major grant, usually a "K" or National Institutes of Health career development award. Fortunately, *The Mentoring Guide* debunks the concept of the monogamous mentor or classic mentor-mentee dyad as outdated. Instead, we are introduced to the concept of team-based mentoring as the new standard. And mentoring teams don't just spread out the work; they actually are most effective when the team includes diverse perspectives in different roles. This is especially true for women and minorities, who face unique issues in career advancement.

This is just a sampling of the high-yield self-help in store for you in *The Mentoring Guide*. Regardless of whether you are an experienced mentor or a first-time mentee, you will gain actionable advice that you can put into practice in your mentoring relationships. You will certainly recognize examples of mentor malpractice, or consider "mentoring tests" to assess mentees. It even tackles taboo topics of how to break up when your mentoring relationship is not working and how to mentor women effectively in the #MeToo era. So, while I may never be your mentor, I hope I have successfully coached you to keep reading.

Vineet Arora, MD, MAPP
Assistant Dean of Scholarship & Discovery
Director of GME Clinical Learning Environment and Innovation
University of Chicago

PREFACE

An impactful, productive career is a result of many different influences in a person's life. Formal education, dedication, and personal study are usually essential ingredients to career success. But another, often overlooked piece—and perhaps the most important one—is mentorship.

But what *exactly* is mentorship? Mentorship is guidance provided by an experienced and trusted incumbent to another (usually junior) individual with the intent to help the junior person succeed. Mentors can be found in every successful organization. The passing of knowledge, strategy, and lived experiences from mentor to mentee through mentorship ensures ongoing achievement and fulfillment in all fields. Take for example the famous chain of mentorship in Greek philosophy: Socrates mentored Plato, who went on to mentor Aristotle. Through his mentees Socrates was able to extend his reach more than he ever would have alone. In this way, the relationship is actually mutually beneficial and bidirectional: mentors gain followers to cement their legacy and ideas, while mentees gain the wisdom needed to perform better than they would have without such guidance. Mentorship is necessary for the success and evolution of a field, ensuring that sagacity is passed on from generation to generation.

In many cases, mentorship is a life-changing experience that bears fruit for years to come. But be aware that approaching mentorship too flippantly or without the full attention it deserves often results in time and energy wasted. Or worse. Mentorship gone awry can lead to regret, destroy relationships, and devastate careers.

Having served as both mentors and mentees, we've seen mentoring relationships succeed and fail. We've talked to numerous mentors and mentees in different fields about their successes and failures. This monograph compiles our stories and experiences with mentoring, as both mentors and mentees, as well as the experiences of many others with whom we've worked throughout our careers.

Our goal is simple: provide actionable, concrete advice that you can use to make the most of your mentoring experiences. We will divulge key steps that good mentors and mentees take to improve the chances of a rewarding outcome. We provide further reading for those interested in learning more about a topic. Finally, we annotate 37 key articles and books about mentorship that will help you review key literature on this vital topic.

We hope the information provided helps you succeed, regardless of whether you are a mentor, a mentee, or somewhere in between.

Vineet Chopra
Valerie M. Vaughn
Sanjay Saint
Ann Arbor, Michigan

ACKNOWLEDGMENTS

This book would not be possible without the help of colleagues, friends, mentees, and mentors from whom we have learned. Our own mentors have influenced us greatly.

For Vineet this list includes Erdal Cavusoglu, Mark Larey, Scott Flanders, Sanjay Saint, Larry McMahon, Bob Wachter, John Carethers, Rod Hayward, and Andy Auerbach.

For Valerie: Vineet Chopra, Sanjay Saint, Scott Flanders, Sarah Krein, Lona Mody, and all the successful women of #FFL who inspire me daily.

For Sanjay: Deb Grady (first research mentor), Larry Tierney (first clinical mentor), Bob Wachter (first career mentor), Steve Fihn, Ben Lipsky, Walt Stamm, Rick Deyo, Tom Koepsell, Larry McMahon, Eve Kerr, Rod Hayward, John Carethers, Gil Omenn, Carol Kauffman, Tim Hofer, and Jim Woolliscroft.

We would also like to acknowledge the University of Michigan and the VA Ann Arbor Healthcare System—two institutions in which mentoring is a core value to be taken seriously.

This book is the combined work of many individuals, and we greatly appreciate the assistance of Jennifer Berry, Jasna Markovac, Jason Mann, Jason Engle, Rachel Ehrlinger, and Michele Mazlin.

Several of the concepts discussed in this book could not have been developed without the help of Dana Edelson, Vinny Arora, Justin Dimick, Jennifer Waljee, Michelle Moniz, and Mary Dixon-Woods. We also thank our artist—Danny Suarez (a student at the Penny W. Stamps School of Art and Design at the University of Michigan)—for providing an inspiring vision of what the art should look like for this book.

PART 1:
FOR MENTORS

Chapter 1
THREE STEPS TO GETTING STARTED AS A MENTOR

Perhaps you never thought of yourself as a mentor, but you're being thrust into the role anyway. Or maybe you've dreamed of mentoring for years and are ready to jump in with both feet. Or maybe you're already a mentor and don't even realize it.

Regardless of your feelings about mentorship, it's a necessary piece of any successful field. And sooner or later, each of us will be asked to step into the role. For some, this might be sooner than expected. Younger fields (like hospital medicine) must cultivate mentors at an earlier stage of their career. For others, mentorship may come later, once a career has been enriched by diverse and varied experiences.

Regardless of timing, becoming well versed in how good mentorship works before becoming a mentor will help both you and your mentee succeed. Most importantly, we want to underscore how fulfilling and rewarding a successful mentoring relationship can be. To this end, we recommend keeping these three basic rules in mind as you begin your journey.

1. TEAM MENTORSHIP IS THE NEW STANDARD

A team of mentors can offer far more than one single mentor, even if that mentor is among the best in their field. Though some may enjoy the ego boost associated with having their very "own" mentee, this isn't the best choice for either party. Indeed, there was once a time when a single mentor took a mentee "under their wing" and claimed sole responsibility for a mentee's success. But in today's sink-or-swim era of team-based problem solving and science, this is neither effective nor prudent for you or your mentee. Why is team based mentoring ideal?

- *The mentee gains a broader perspective.* Different personalities, work styles, and opportunities for learning must come from multiple people. A single mentor teaches only their way of doing things, depriving the mentee of important exposure to diversity, creativity, and problem-solving ability. Not to mention, mentors may have varying clinical or methodological skills, career experiences, and content expertise. Having more than one mentor fosters development of bigger networks and more valuable connections—all of which are key to mentee success.

- *The mentor gets a more manageable workload.* We would argue that few have the time and resources to truly invest in a mentee the way they deserve without help from others. In fact, those with plenty of time on their hands are often *unbusy* for a reason. We often half-jokingly tell our colleagues, "If you want something done, ask someone who is busy to do it." This is because most such people are busy for a reason: they are exceptionally good at what they do and almost always accomplish what they pursue. Thus, many would-be ideal mentors are stretched to the max with their own professional and personal commitments. Having a mentorship team, instead of exclusively taking on a mentee, spreads workload around, helping you avoid neglecting other necessary responsibilities or, even worse, burning out.

· **Both parties gain a safety net for unforeseen circumstances.** Today's workforce is more mobile than ever before. A mentor may decide to leave their job or institution for any number of reasons. A solo mentor thus could leave the mentee in a lurch that damages not only their learning process but possibly their future career path. Similarly, a mentor may have poured resources and hours into a mentee—only to have the mentee leave for personal or professional reasons. The mentor is, of course, conflicted. On the one hand, they are happy to see the mentee leave for a better opportunity. On the other hand, the mentor may be disappointed that another organization is now the beneficiary of the countless hours spent on grooming a budding star.

What's more, a team of mentors helps inoculate against mentorship malpractice—mentor behaviors that jeopardize the mentee's chance of success (discussed in **Chapters 6 and 7**). And mentorship teams may actually help the mentor grow connections and relationships with other members of the team, especially those outside of their field. An example: a medical school faculty member mentoring a mentee with a nursing background can now meet and collaborate with nursing faculty who are also on the mentoring committee.

2. INITIATE A TRIAL RUN

It's a truism that we observe even starting in preschool: some people you immediately click with, others not so much. And this basic human tendency must be considered before any mentoring relationship is created. Remember, a positive mentoring relationship needs to have all-around good "chemistry." It's not just about personality types or how much someone "likes" another person. It's about finding the right fit in terms of work ethic, expectations, knowledge, and temperament. But be on the lookout for possible "implicit bias"—is your negative reaction to the mentee rooted in the fact that they may not look or act like you? Heuristics—or mental shortcuts—are powerful and automatic; being mindful (discussed more fully in **Chapter 3**) may help guard against this very human failing.

Before agreeing to mentor an individual, carefully consider the person who will be your mentee. Remember that you'll be sacrificing your own professional time and personal energy to help this person succeed. Thus, this is hardly a decision to be taken lightly.

Look for someone who is ambitious and organized but also independent and flexible. Many mentor-mentee relationships have gone sour because a mentee was calling their mentor with every little question or every time they encountered a bump in the road. Others have failed because one party didn't do their part to keep the communication lines open or wasn't tolerant of perspectives that differed from their own.

Most importantly, ask yourself: can I *trust* this person? Whether it is concerns over scientific conduct or maintaining the integrity of private and confidential discussions, the mentor should not take on a mentee that they do not trust (the converse is true as well). Though it is rare, several examples exist of mentees that have committed academic fraud, thereby undermining both their careers and the careers of their mentors.

But how does one choose the right protégé? Choosing the right mentee may be as simple as doing a "trial run" before you commit. Try one of the following approaches to get a feel for the mentee's fit, dedication, and knowledge before you say "yes" to mentorship.

The Reading Test

Ask your prospective mentee to read a book or paper that you find particularly influential in your field. Then ask them to set up another meeting in a month or so with you to discuss their take on it. Nine out of ten will never be heard from again.

If a mentee is willing to take the time to read, interpret, and discuss the paper with you, you know the mentee has an appetite for learning and is committed. The discussion is also a welcome opportunity to listen to their ideas and decide whether they have the knowledge, passion, and initiative needed to move forward (without too much hand-holding). On the other hand, if they don't make that follow-up appointment or show up with half-baked or half-prepared answers, you may have saved yourself months of pain. Be especially wary of potential mentees who make the follow-up appointment but don't do the assignment due to various excuses. To paraphrase Benjamin Franklin, "Show me someone who is very good at excuses, and I will show you someone very good at little else."

The Writing Assignment

As the American author David McCullough has said, "Writing is thinking. To write well is to think clearly. That's why it's so hard." Even when one doesn't feel it's their strong suit, a writing exercise is a good way to assess how a prospective mentee thinks. It also helps demonstrate a mentee's pluck and willingness to learn.

We therefore have asked prospective mentees to write a review of a landmark or key article in their field or even a brief thought-piece about a controversial topic. It doesn't need to be a term paper: we ask for a one- or two-pager and give them a deadline with expectations around content and word count. Like the book test, the writing assignment provides insight into their ideas, thought process, and philosophies. It also helps determine whether they are a closer: someone who finishes what they start.

On-the-Job Test Run

In the management world, it often makes sense to take a mentee with you on a sales call or to a client meeting. A debrief with your mentee after such a meeting can be another opportunity to assess their readiness for this journey. Sit down with your mentee to discuss the interaction or ask them to write up a summary with their thoughts and impressions. This gives you both a chance to see the other in a real-world scenario and to talk about the experience. Not in management? No problem—have them fly along with you in a committee meeting or a stakeholder convention. The same rules apply. If your mentee puts in sincere effort and acts appropriately during the "test," this is a positive sign.

Gain Collateral Information

Rather than relying solely on these tests and your own "gut instinct," an approach at least one of us uses is obtaining collateral information from those who have worked with the possible mentee. For example, for a mentee who is a physician in training (usually referred to as a "house officer" or subspecialty "fellow"), we would ask those who worked most closely with them in the clinical setting—such as their peers, supervisors, nursing staff, social workers—what they were like in a team setting. Specifically, did they return pages from nurses in a timely manner? Did they come to evaluate unstable patients at the bedside when asked to do so? Were they hardworking? Thoughtful? Kind? Did they get along well with colleagues? Any red—or even yellow—flags in terms of ethical behavior? Would you want them to care for a family member? For job candidates who may simultaneously be seeking us out for mentorship once they are hired, we ask the administrative assistant who escorts them to their several one-on-one interviews what their thoughts are on the candidate. We have found that those who "kiss up" often "kick down"—indeed, the person presumably lowest on the organizational ladder will often get a surprisingly accurate sense of what someone is really like. One negative comment, of course, would not derail things; you are looking for a pattern of behavior that makes you question whether they are someone who you want to entrust with your reputation.

At this point, you may wonder, "Does choosing a mentee need to be this difficult and time-consuming?" The answer is "no," provided you are fine with spending time on a mentoring relationship gone awry. We have learned (and know of countless examples) of bad outcomes that will dwarf the time that these upfront suggestions will take. And perhaps more importantly, doing the hard work now may avoid failed relationships that not only take up time but also reduce your willingness to mentor in the future.

A working relationship with a mentee can last a lifetime. Best to choose wisely.

3. MAKE A GAME PLAN

As with any relationship in life, the key to longevity is open communication and matching expectations. The same follows for mentees. Once you've selected your mentee, establish ground rules of mentorship. This is crucial to making communication and interactions both positive and efficient. Your discussion should establish:

- Your mentee's short- and long-term goals. And these should be revisited regularly, since people's goals may change over time.
- A regular meeting cadence, time, and place to cover progress, roadblocks, and questions.
- What constitutes an urgent matter that may need to be discussed outside of your regular meetings (but best keep these to a minimum).
- What services you will provide to your mentee (and conversely, what you will not).
- Your expectations from your mentee regarding professional behavior, quality of work, and specific milestones they should accomplish.
- The tone and expectations about dealing with mistakes and problems. You don't expect perfection (mentees are still learning), but you do expect honesty and willingness to find solutions. When mistakes are made or your mentee encounters problems, they should be upfront and timely and have a plan to deal with it.

Another important aspect to a successful mentoring relationship is trust, ideally for both parties. A zone of safety—and confidentiality—for discussing aspects that are sensitive will exist during mentoring sessions. In short, your mentee should feel comfortable bringing these issues to your attention, and you as the mentor, in turn, should feel comfortable in providing candid advice with the assumption that such information will not be taken out of context. This may become tricky, however, when the mentor wears more than one hat. For example, a mentor who also has major leadership responsibilities in the organization may not be able to keep certain matters private if they put others at risk—such as if the mentee mentions during a mentoring session that a physician colleague is drinking alcohol while on clinical duty or a colleague is behaving unethically or illegally.

Practically speaking, at the outset of every new mentoring relationship, we recommend a regular meeting every two to four weeks. You should ask mentees to draft an agenda for these meetings, outlining where they are with projects, what their current needs are, and what questions or discussion points they would like to cover. Make sure you require mentees to send agendas to you several days in advance so you can prepare for the meeting and add or modify items if needed. This approach has helped us become better mentors, and we have found it helps train the mentee to use their time with us wisely.

Finally, be very clear on defining what constitutes egregious errors and how you will handle them. Plagiarism, scientific misconduct, abusive conduct, and the like should be listed as grounds to end the relationship and may result in disciplinary action. If the mentee knows this up front, there can be no question later about what the consequences are should these unfortunate issues arise.

SUMMARY

Mentorship requires preparation and thought before the first step has been taken. As Benjamin Franklin said, "An ounce of prevention is worth a pound of cure." While you'll be using some of your valuable time and energy to select the mentee and to establish ground rules, these critical steps could save you countless hours of stress and wasted resources later.

Beginning mentorship on the right foot not only helps improve the outcome of this relationship but ensures that both you and your mentee can reap the benefits of this mutual—and hopefully rewarding—experience. Ultimately, this will allow mentees to learn more, lead to higher mutual satisfaction, and enable you both to contribute even more value to your organization and field.

TAKE-HOME POINTS

- Don't keep a mentee to yourself: create a team of mentors to maximize benefits for all involved parties.
- Don't start mentoring someone prematurely; wait for the right time and the right mentee.
- Give your mentee "tests" before committing and seek out collateral information to assess "fit."
- Communication is key; always start by setting clear expectations and ground rules.

Chapter 2
KNOW YOUR ROLE

There is no "standard issue" when it comes to mentoring: each mentor-mentee dyad is a unique partnership. Every mentor brings something different to the table based upon their own strengths, identity, and background. This is a good thing because mentees benefit from different types of leaders throughout their career.

The key is to know exactly what you can offer to a prospective mentee. In this way, you can better determine how you both may benefit from the partnership. There are four archetypes and roles to consider.

THE TRADITIONAL MENTOR

The traditional mentor is invested in the long-term growth of a mentee. They offer frequent communication and regular meetings to help the mentee grow in their specific discipline. Traditional mentors are typified by deep content or methodological knowledge—often in the same field as their mentee.

This type of mentoring requires acute attention to detail and a considerable investment of time to ensure the mentee is producing high-quality work and is on track for success. Mentors and mentees in this arrangement thrive on respect and trust, akin to the relationship between a high-performing employee and boss or expert and apprentice.

The end goal of a traditional mentor partnership is to ensure the mentee acquires the skill and knowledge needed to succeed on their own. In fact, that is how the success of the relationship is measured. A traditional mentor is, therefore, a guide who will nurture and advocate for their mentee much like a parent may for a child.

THE COACH

Unlike mentors, coaches are not necessarily invested in the long-term success of a mentee. Rather, coaches help mentees improve performance in one domain or solve a specific issue that they are grappling with.

Coaching, therefore, does not involve the same degree of time or energy as a traditional mentorship. It is often a "one-off" type of relationship, though it can recur several times with the same or different people through a mentee's career. The bottom line is that coaches always come in to provide specific help for specific issues—and then they are gone. For instance, a coach may be particularly adept at strategy (such as negotiating job searches or contracts), a specific methodology (e.g., qualitative analysis), or a focused talk (preparing a terrific presentation).

A coach can take on several different mentees at once due to the smaller time commitment. Coaches can provide the best experience to their mentees by being clear about the amount of time they are able to commit and the area in which they can assist their mentee.

Coaching can be done one-on-one or in a small group when several people desire the same type of advice. A coach's limited role means they are usually not the primary mentor for the particular mentee seeking their advice. Nevertheless, their contributions can be vital to a mentee's success.

THE SPONSOR

Sponsors don't generally provide advice or guidance as a traditional mentor or coach may. Rather, a sponsor uses their sphere of influence in a field to help propel or aid a mentee.

For example, sponsors may help their mentee land a spot in a national panel or be selected as a speaker at a key meeting. Sponsors could also help a mentee by writing a letter of recommendation for a job position or membership in an honorific society. In other words, they use their political capital to benefit the mentee. In return, sponsors can strengthen their legacy as identifying and promoting "stars" and ensuring the success of their field.

It's for this last reason that we recommend, if you're going to be a sponsor, choosing your mentees carefully. You risk your own reputation when you recommend someone for an academic or business endeavor. After all, each of us has a limited amount of social and political capital; we should spend it wisely. You want to choose someone who has proven to be a worthy candidate, not someone who is struggling to find their stride or may be an unsure bet. A sponsor must carefully evaluate the success potential of a mentee using both objective metrics (such as publications, grants, sales targets, previous accomplishments) as well as subjective feedback (from those with whom the mentee has worked).

Unfortunately, sponsorship is not equally distributed. Underrepresented minorities are far less likely to be sponsored or identify someone who acts as a sponsor. Lack of sponsorship may partially explain the continued leadership gap between men and women and other minorities despite an increase at entry-level positions in many fields. As a sponsor, keep in mind the human tendency to sponsor people who look (or act or think) like us—or the leaders we're surrounded by. Be cognizant of who you sponsor and strive to nominate men *and* women, traditional *and* nontraditional leaders, and those who may otherwise be underrepresented. After all, unique viewpoints increase creativity and lead to contributions that can be extremely valuable.

Mentees should remember what motivates potential sponsors: using their considerable and earned influence to showcase new talent, help others who are working hard to establish themselves, and advance the field. As a sponsor, you don't necessarily need to tell your mentee, then, that you've supported or recommended them for specific tasks. But a mentee may seek you out—and you should know what to look for and whether it's worth the risk.

THE CONNECTOR

Connectors have unique value. They are the hubs through which a mentee can be paired with the right mentor, coach, or sponsor. They are expert networkers, with a vast array of contacts gained as a result of their own success, charisma, or eminence in a field. While they may not have the bandwidth or desire to mentor in the traditional sense, they are motivated by seeing the field succeed and strongly believe in creating a nurturing pipeline for prospective stars. They may also simply like to help others.

Connectors are valuable to mentees, mentors, and their field at large. For example, a connector helps mentees succeed by introducing them to mentors, sponsors, or coaches. Similarly, connectors help mentors by identifying prospective talent or defining areas for coaching or people for sponsorship. In doing these activities, connectors help ensure that their field continues to attract and retain effective and influential people.

Where can you find connectors? Such individuals are often in a senior leadership role that lends itself to affiliations and connections beyond their organization. They tend to be department heads, C-suite members, or in charge of external networks within the organization. They have reached positions of prominence and influence, often related to the help they have received along the way from other connectors. They thus thrive on tapping into their extensive network to promote new people in the field. If you need a connector, look up the org chart—you're likely to find a few there. But don't overlook people just because they are relatively junior in the organization. We know of several easygoing, extroverted, and influential individuals who seem to know everyone at national meetings and who are relatively junior in their fields. These are individuals who can also make an introduction on your behalf to someone in their vast network.

SUMMARY

A mentor's role can take many different forms: traditional mentor, coach, sponsor, or connector. At some stage, you may have to play all or some of these roles for a mentee. At any given time, you may be one role for many mentees or many roles for one mentee.

We know from our own experiences that we have turned to—and benefited from—all four of these mentor phenotypes at some stage. Mentees will need to determine what they need for their growth and then must seek it out. As a mentor, fulfilling these varied roles makes you more valuable and respected. Thus, these four archetypes are important not just for the success of a mentee, but for a mentor and the field as well.

TAKE-HOME POINTS

- Mentorship should be based upon matching what the mentee needs and what the mentor(s) can offer.
- The traditional mentor guides a mentee toward success and growth with a significant time commitment.
- The coach offers expertise on a specific area of focus or project.
- The sponsor uses their influence to recommend a mentee for opportunities and/or projects.
- The connector focuses on pairing up mentors and mentees through strong social networks and influence.

Chapter 3
SIX RULES FOR
MINDFUL MENTORING

Mentors have power over their mentees because they usually have greater training and professional experience. Often mentors also have administrative or leadership roles, giving them additional power relative to mentees. Typically, this power is used for the mentee's benefit (e.g., sponsorship, negotiation). Unfortunately, some mentors use this as an opportunity to take advantage of their mentees' lesser status and vulnerability.

Mindful mentoring means that you honor the virtues of integrity and honesty that are crucial to productive and ethical mentorship. Many mentors wear various "hats" in an organization. In addition to being someone's research mentor, they may serve as an executive within the organization. The "hat" they wear may influence the advice they provide the mentee. There may be situations when your best interests may not align with that of your mentee. For example, a mentee may have a wonderful professional opportunity that takes them away from you or your company. In this case, you have to wear your "mentor's hat" and think about what is best for the mentee (not necessarily what is best for you or your organization). If you are also the mentee's division chief, you may then say something like "I am now going to take off my mentor's hat and put on my division chief's hat and let you know why I think you should consider staying." We suggest the following approach: first, be honest—let the mentee know you have a conflict of interest. Second, tell them your opinion given your conflict of interest (e.g., I don't want to see you go). Then, try to give them advice as if no conflict existed (e.g., it's a wonderful opportunity, and you need to think about whether it makes sense for you and your family).

Mindful mentoring draws heavily on the concept of "mindfulness," in which you are fully present and engaged in the here and now. Here are six rules for mindful mentoring that we try to follow to ensure a fruitful experience for both parties.

RULE 1: GIVE CREDIT TO YOUR MENTEE

Mentoring is not about recognition for you: it's about passing on experience and knowledge to your mentee. Celebrate the achievements and efforts of your mentee and always give them the credit they deserve. The traditional approach is to do this in person or at meetings with a "shout-out" about your mentee. Increasingly, however, new and creative ways are important. For example, we often go to our mentee's presentation, take a picture of them at the podium, and put out a congratulatory comment on our social media feed, mentioning—and tagging—them. Sometimes, we send out an email lauding an award that our mentee received (or a major paper that they published) to the department chair or other senior leaders in our organization who may not have known about the mentee's accomplishment. One of the key duties of a mentor is to brag about the mentee so they do not feel compelled to brag about themselves (which should be avoided, if at all possible). After all, a competent and successful mentee is a positive reflection on you as well.

RULE 2: GIVE YOUR MENTEE DUTIES THAT ARE BENEFICIAL TO THEIR GROWTH, NOT YOURS

A mentee is not there to manage your projects or to make your job easier by completing tasks you don't have time to address. Any assignments your mentee receives from you, and any task that they take on independently, should thus be of benefit to them before anyone else.

This isn't to say they can't work on projects that are of interest to you or those on which you are the leader. However, they should walk away from their effort on the projects being the better for it. And, of course, they should be offered the opportunity to work on the project and can then decide if it is something that interests them. Resist the temptation to pressure them to do something—it is short-term gain that usually leads to long-term pain.

Before we assign tasks to mentees, we ask ourselves, "Does this help my mentee learn and grow in their area of expertise?" If we can't answer "yes" immediately, we reconsider or reframe the assignment. After all, when they grow, we do too.

RULE 3: ALLOW YOUR MENTEE TO BRANCH OUT

In **Chapter 1**, we shared how a mentee learns best from a variety of mentors. But we know some mentors—especially those who are insecure—prefer not sharing mentees. Rather, they tend to lure their mentee (either deliberately or inadvertently) into an "exclusive relationship," isolating and preventing them from seeking advice or partnerships with others. We believe that this is both an unhealthy and unproductive approach.

For one, it limits a mentee's growth and their ability to learn different approaches, styles, and strategies from others. Second, it makes the mentee reliant on you for everything—often leading to a high volume of communication and meetings. And third, it limits your growth as a mentor to learn from cross-pollination of knowledge from other experts in the mentee's field.

Encourage your mentee to take risks and connect with others. If nothing else, it will save you time. Best-case scenario: it may prove to be highly beneficial to your mentee and you.

RULE 4: KEEP THINGS MOVING

You must have the time and desire to meet regularly with your mentee, answer their questions, and ensure their projects are moving forward. This means you must be willing to sacrifice some of your own time and energy to make this happen. If your mentee must seek your approval for a paper, grant, or client interaction, be sure you get back with them in a timely manner. Mentors who insist on being engaged at every step but make mentees wait for several days or even weeks for a response become an obstacle to success. Don't be that mentor.

We highlight this as a rule because it is helpful to remember that the mentee's timeline is usually different than yours. It is usually shorter. You are already established and are a known (and hopefully valuable) entity to your organization. Your mentee, on the other hand, must prove themselves and often must do so relatively quickly (e.g., during their internship or probationary start-up period). This is especially true for looming deadlines like grant submissions or major presentations that will require your feedback.

Delays disproportionately and adversely affect the mentee, and good mentors must seek to accelerate, not slow down, success.

RULE 5: BE READY FOR DIFFICULT CONVERSATIONS

The close relationship that develops between a mentor and mentee means some disagreements are inevitable. A key rule of mentorship, therefore, is to expect rifts and be prepared to manage them.

You'll need to develop comfort in approaching your mentee to discuss sensitive issues in a professional manner with a goal of honest resolution. You do no one a favor if you try to be a friend instead of a mentor. Be calm but direct. And if your mentee has made a critical error, be clear about steps that must be taken to correct the problem as well as the timeline in which these should happen. Never leave a mentee guessing as to what they should do when something goes horribly awry. A little preparation ahead of time goes a long way.

We know that these conversations are never easy, so we offer this piece of wisdom: a good mentor should separate the person from the issue. Thank the mentee for their candor. And end by reemphasizing your belief in their character and abilities. But have no qualms about addressing the issues as you see them unfold. Do so with firmness, clarity, and empathy. Effective mentors focus on what matters and dissect the issues while realizing that candor without kindness amounts to cruelty. And these difficult conversations should take place in a private setting—never publicly.

As we wrote in *Harvard Business Review*,

> Before meetings with mentees (especially ones where difficult feedback or conversations may happen), we consciously try to put ourselves in their shoes before and during the conversation. This has made us more empathetic and compassionate in our roles

as mentors. Making it as a junior physician or budding academician is hard. Established leaders lose sight of this and forget the struggles that their mentees face. By putting ourselves in the role of the mentees—and doing so purposefully several times during our interactions—we have learned to take the edge off the sometimes-difficult advice we provide. When critiquing our student's suboptimal case presentation, for example, we think to ourselves "they are doing the best they can" and provide feedback accordingly.

RULE 6: BE AVAILABLE

The paradox about success is that as it comes a mentor's way, their ability to engage in the work that made them so successful becomes limited. Many professionals thus find themselves caught in a whirlwind of meetings, speaking engagements, and travel that dominate their time. Such a demanding schedule is an obstacle to fulfilling your obligations as a mentor. We suggest the following approaches to work around these challenges:

- *Try shorter meetings.* Who says all mentor meetings have to be 45 or 60 minutes? We have found incredible utility in the 30-minute (and, occasionally, the 20-minute) meeting rather than a 60-minute traditional block of mentoring. And shorter time blocks might also help your mentoring relationship—it forces mentees to get to their key concerns right away and requires you to be concise in your response. Thus, it could be good for both of you!
- *Be creative.* Simple touch points can be just as helpful as longer mentoring meetings. A quick phone call on the weekend,

text message, or brief email after hours can help a mentee stay on track while allowing you to get other things done during the workday.

· **Technology is your friend.** Just because you are in a different time zone or hemisphere does not mean you cannot communicate. Video conferencing and telephones are good options. And if you are on travels with your mentee, use travel time to your advantage. We've had mentoring sessions at 30,000 feet, in an airport lounge, and beyond!

· **Be realistic about what you can do.** Decide whether your hectic life truly allows the time and mental and emotional energy required to mentor someone who will rely upon your expertise—and your presence—on a regular basis.

· **But don't overlook perhaps the most important aspect of this rule.** Be present and fully engaged with the conversation regardless of what else may be going on. Just because you are *able* to speak with your mentee (in person, over the phone, or via FaceTime or Skype) does not mean that you are actually *communicating* in a meaningful way. This is particularly relevant if you find yourself distracted during the conversation (thinking about all the tasks that are piling up) or trying to multitask (by also checking your emails) while putatively providing guidance to someone in need of your wisdom. This also holds during regularly scheduled routine meetings in your office with your mentee: fully engage by showing them that for the next 30 minutes, they are all that matters.

SUMMARY

Mindful mentoring is more than just a catchphrase. The practice requires benevolence, self-reflection, and self-improvement. It requires that the mentor be fully present during conversations and interactions with the mentee, regardless of where and how those interactions occur.

Too many times, mentorship is viewed as a ticket to popularity or as something you "have to do," without particular attention to the responsibility and importance the role entails. Mentorship may be difficult, but it should also be fulfilling. You have a wonderful opportunity to shape another professional *and* all of their future mentees as well. By following the six rules of mindful mentoring, we hope you can become the best possible mentor you can be. Your mentee—and your field—depend on it.

TAKE-HOME POINTS

- Good mentors realize that mentorship is not about their own gratification and glory but about helping their mentees find success.
- Don't make your mentee rely upon you for everything—and when you do need to provide key guidance, do it quickly so your mentee can keep moving.
- Be ready to address disagreements or uncomfortable situations quickly and directly when they happen, and do so in a candid yet kind manner.
- Shorter, more efficient meetings; modern technology; and some creativity can help you fit more into your schedule.
- Be present in the moment. Dedicate your full attention to the conversation at hand . . . and most of all, enjoy the experience, as mentor- and menteeship can be invigorating!

PART 2:

Chapter 4
THE MENTEE'S
QUICK-START GUIDE

Though some may assume that the mentor bears the main load of responsibility in a mentorship, this is far from the truth. Just as the secret to good leadership is good followership, the hallmark of a successful mentor-mentee relationship is an engaged, productive, and trustworthy mentee.

A critical mistake on the part of the mentee is the failure to recognize that they must bring their "A" game to the relationship. Without their best effort, the relationship can quickly deteriorate and contribute to career difficulties. A once-promising career can even be blunted as a consequence. Additionally, mentees may lose a salient opportunity for growth and enlightenment—which may affect not only their career but that of the mentors and the field as a whole.

Despite these facts, most articles about mentorship are often focused on what the mentor should do. They neglect to mention that mentees have a crucial role in this balance and thus also must have a defined strategy for success. Like mentors, mentees need a playbook by which they can plan and evaluate their growth. Given the asymmetrical nature of the relationship, mentees have more to lose than their mentors if the mentoring relationship is problematic. So here are some of the steps we share with our mentees to ensure they develop a rewarding relationship.

CHOOSE YOUR MENTOR WISELY

Just as a mentor chooses the right mentee, you also should be selective about your potential mentor. Being careless about mentor selection could be professionally harmful to you. This is especially true of your "traditional mentor"—criteria for sponsors, coaches, and connectors can be looser.

How do you know if a mentor is a good fit? We suggest asking yourself these questions about a prospective mentor:

1. Is this a person I can see myself becoming one day?
2. Are they professional, trustworthy, and approachable? Do they have integrity?
3. Do their skills, priorities, and expertise line up with my career goals?
4. Does this person seem to have a genuine desire to mentor me?
5. Are their prior mentees doing well today? Have they had positive experiences with this mentor? (If you don't know, ask them!)

If you answer "no" to any of these questions, we strongly suggest reconsidering whether the mentor is right for you. It is far better to delay or change your decision in choosing a mentor in order to find the right person than to try to extract a positive result from a poorly matched connection.

BE MINDFUL OF YOUR MENTOR'S TIME—STARTING NOW

If you've chosen exceptional mentors, there's a good chance that they have a lot on their plates. In fact, a good rule of thumb is that your mentor is often three times busier than you think they are. After all, most great mentors are accomplished and, as such, possess many roles and responsibilities that demand their time. The best ones make it look relatively easy, but trust us—it is not.

Despite their packed schedules, they are enthusiastic about investing their time into mentoring you. Great! But being willing to help doesn't mean they have a surplus of time to hand-hold or discuss minor details. Always treat your mentors' time as a precious resource that should be used wisely and productively.

How can you ensure that you get the best use of each moment with your mentor and avoid wasting their time?

- **Schedule recurrent meetings.** This not only solidifies your valuable face-to-face time with your mentor but skips the hassle of calling an assistant to find an open time or frivolous emails back and forth to set up an appointment. You and each of your mentors should agree upon a regular rotation of meetings—and stick to it.
- **Prepare for each meeting.** You want each minute to be spent on the topics you need help with now. Create an agenda of items and prioritize what's most important. One trick we have used—especially when a mentor tends to be verbose

or easily distracted by tangents—is to schedule the amount of time to spend on each topic within the meeting. This helps keep you on task and avoids you (or your mentor) wandering off into topics that you could handle outside of the meeting.

- **Bring your thoughts to the table.** Your mentor wants to hear how you might handle a given situation or challenge. Rather than coming in blank and relying upon your mentor for every answer, craft one or two possible solutions and strategies and ask them what they think. This not only shows initiative; it gives them an opportunity to help you improve on your approach. And importantly, it helps you grow as you learn to modify your approach through advice from your mentor. In fact, most effective mentors (or supervisors) we know usually ask the following question when presented with a dilemma: "What do you suggest we should do?"

- **Tell your mentor what to expect.** Several days before your regular meeting, send an email with your agenda and anything you would like your mentor to do in advance to make the most of your time together. For instance, you may ask your mentor to read through an abstract, article, or PowerPoint presentation so you can get feedback during your meeting. Having a mentor read this during your face-to-face meeting is a waste of their time—and yours.

LEARN HOW TO RUN EFFICIENT MEETINGS

It can be nerve-wracking to prepare a meeting with your mentor present, especially if it's a new partnership. But the agenda doesn't have to be complicated. Include the following topics, and you'll find that your meetings provide a time of maximum productivity and learning for both of you.

- Progress toward goals since your last meeting (or simply stating your goals if it's your first meeting).
- New projects you are considering—and whether or not you should engage in them (be prepared for listing the pros/cons of each).
- Updates on customer or client connections or journal and grant correspondence.
- A brief summary of what you're working on now and any obstacles you are facing.
- How things are going from their perspective with the mentoring relationship (perhaps even asking them if, for example, they recommend modifications to the meeting schedule, agenda items, or frequency of communications).

If you're following the guidelines listed here for your meetings, you will find that lengthy conversations outside of the meeting are usually unnecessary. But sometimes urgent matters come up that may require your mentor's advice or approval to move forward. When this happens, be sure you know the protocol for getting in touch with your mentor.

Our approach is to ask our mentees to send a succinct email (with the subject line indicating the topic and time sensitivity, if appropriate) with their question or concern clearly called out for any communication. We ask them to use an "elevator speech" technique: imagine you have 30 seconds to tell us about the issue and get our response—how would you do that? Start with a bolded question you want your mentor to answer followed by two to three short sentences of background that might be needed for the decision. Avoid the alternative—a lengthy message with vague questions embedded within it. The former setup makes it easier for your mentor to address the issue during two minutes of free time. You're more likely to get a quick answer. And it allows the mentor to reply using their handheld mobile device with a simple yes or no.

SUMMARY

Like mentorship, menteeship is a practice that must be learned over time. Highly effective mentees jump-start their careers by choosing the right mentor and using their skills in a respectful way.

Being thoughtful about how and when communication occurs, preparing for meetings to maximize benefit, and becoming highly organized are just a few key skills you will benefit from learning during this period of time. Acquiring these practices will help you become not only a productive mentee but also a highly sought-after mentor in the future.

TAKE-HOME POINTS

- As a mentee, you are just as accountable as the mentor for the success of your relationship; in fact, you have more to lose if things go poorly.
- Prudent mentor selection is crucial to a productive mentorship.
- Treat your mentor's time like a valuable resource that should be spent wisely.
- Taking the time to prepare for your meetings will allow you to get much more accomplished in a short amount of time.
- When reaching out to your mentor outside of regular meetings or via email, use yes/no questions and provide a brief background to quickly get the answers you need.

Chapter 5
NINE THINGS STANDOUT
MENTEES DO

You have your own goals, work ethic, and personality. You don't have to sacrifice your individuality to make your time as a mentee as rewarding as possible. However, there are several qualities that we've seen time and again that increase the odds of success for mentees. Combine these guidelines with your own knowledge and drive, and you've got a roadmap for success.

1. ***Begin with an honest conversation.*** Honesty begins with yourself. What are your goals? What is your mission? Who do you want to be in 10, 20, 40 years? Then, continue that conversation with your mentor. Show your mentor that you're serious about making the most of this relationship by crafting a written plan of your short- and long-term goals. Send the plan to your mentor in advance of your first standing meeting. This can be daunting. But remember, it serves multiple purposes. First, it helps you determine whether a shared vision of success exists; second, it helps your mentor

advise you (or sponsor you) in a way that fits your goals; and third, it helps clarify roles and expectations for both of you. This simple step can spare you disagreement (or worse, disappointment) later.

You may even consider going a step further. Before meeting with prospective mentors, send (ideally several days before) a copy of your CV and a one-page overview of your accomplishments and goals. In this way, the conversation can focus on their thoughts on your future rather than you reciting your past to them. It also provides your mentor with the opportunity to consider more carefully the prospect of taking you on as a mentee. Even if they don't end up being your mentor, you will likely get helpful and thoughtful feedback, since they will have mulled it over before meeting you.

2. *Always keep your mentor in the loop.* A mentor can't help you if you're not being candid about your efforts and what you're trying to achieve. Being vague or too broad about your activities and endeavors only serves to set you up for failure and will likely frustrate your mentor. Remember your mentor is highly connected. There's nothing worse than for them to learn of your involvement with something through someone else—especially if that activity detracts from what you should be working on (or what they thought you were working on!). Relatedly, we recommend checking with your mentor before committing to new tasks or new opportunities, especially if these are likely going to require substantial time.

3. *Be open about obstacles.* All good mentors know you will run into difficulties and make mistakes. But if you don't discuss your concerns or missteps, you're missing out on

a prime opportunity to gain problem-solving skills from your mentor. Remember, the odds are high that your mentor likely encountered some of these same issues when they were in your position. We recommend trying to bring one problem or concern to each face-to-face meeting in order to help you grow as a mentee. These may range from "Should I go to this meeting?" to "I'm having difficulties balancing work and life." Bringing the smaller issues to the table can be very valuable in building trust to manage the big ones when they arise. Most importantly, don't try to hide major problems from your mentor for fear that they may think of you unfavorably. If one of these "red flag" events occurs—for example, accusations of plagiarism or scientific misconduct, or you have become embroiled in a bitter personal battle with someone at work—let your mentor know as soon as you can. Keeping them in the dark will only make things worse. Your mentor can serve as a key advocate and ally during times of duress. At the very least, they can provide perspective and advice on handling thorny situations because they either have confronted something similar themselves or have seen such a situation before. Remember, it is rare that a seasoned and effective mentor will be caught completely off guard by something you tell them.

4. **Listen more than you talk.** Remember that the main purpose of menteeship is to learn from someone who is more experienced and seasoned than you. It may be tempting to try to fill the time with your personal accomplishments or your views on how things should be done. Don't do this. Remember, when you are the one talking, you are not learning anything new. We have even coined a term for the

importance of this rule—we refer to this as "Talking to Listening Ratio (TLR)." The goal is to ensure that your TLR is less than 1; that is, make sure you are talking less than your mentor by practicing the art of not interrupting. Preparing for meetings ahead of time with agendas is a key strategy to accomplishing this goal. Another tactic is to pay attention to when you want to interrupt; rather than doing so, force yourself to wait until your mentor is finished to say something. You may even find that the burning retort or interjection is no longer applicable.

5. *Focus on being professional.* As a mentee, you're probably new to the field, and others are forming an impression of you. Your mentor and others are not likely to respond well to drama, complaining, or gossiping. While emotions indicate passion and enthusiasm, frequent emotional outbursts can tarnish your reputation early in your career. Focus on being positive and poised, especially when setbacks (of which there will be many) come your way. And learn how to take constructive criticism with grace. After all, this feedback is for your benefit, not your mentors. We cannot stress this enough: an effective way to churn through mentors is to be defensive when they provide feedback. Their feedback should be treated as a gift rather than a personal attack. While some mentors may enjoy bullying, humiliating, or demeaning their mentees, we have found that this type of behavior is uncommon. Giving feedback requires time and effort and typically means your mentor has your best interests at heart. If you find yourself in the unenviable position of having a jerk as a mentor, end the relationship as quickly and as amicably as you can.

6. **Follow through.** When you say you'll do something, no matter how minor, do it. Even small, seemingly trivial projects could be a strike against you if you let them fall through the cracks. Have a system for recording all your tasks and promised to-do's and check daily to be sure you're not letting anything slip. Many effective mentees keep weekly task lists of things that they need to work on, breaking down large projects (e.g., grants or customer accounts) into smaller components or steps. When you always do what you say you'll do, others will appreciate your reliability and will want to invite you to further opportunities.

7. **Lose the "me" mentality.** As a mentee, you are learning to grow in your skills to one day become an ideal mentor. One such skill is learning to give others credit where it is due and to do so generously and graciously. If you become known as a team player, you increase your chances of being a part of future group opportunities that will enrich your professional pursuits. This is often hard for mentees to learn, since they are trying to establish themselves and their reputations. They often become internally focused in this quest, shunning potential opportunities to assist others in fear that it will detract from their own pursuits. Our advice is to lose the "me" mentality whenever possible. It pays dividends in the long run. Pay attention to what others do and say and how they behave—and remind yourself that others are paying the same attention to you. Helping out—even a little bit—goes a long way.

8. **Underpromise and overdeliver.** What you do (or don't do) directly reflects on you and your abilities. Always put forth your best work, and give yourself ample time to do

it so you can turn it in ahead of schedule. Don't try to cram something in when you're swamped, and be honest with yourself if you are. We tell mentees to ask for more than the time they need to do a job well but still try to finish early. This behavior is closely linked to "following through" but specifically includes doing the job well and ahead of schedule. Endeavor to be the mentee who under-promises and overdelivers. Once you have this reputation, it will serve you well. The opposite—overpromising while underdelivering—can sink careers.

9. ***Don't lose sight of your goals.*** If you feel you're being asked to do projects that don't align with your goals, speak up. Talk to your mentor first and discuss how or why these tasks are ending up on your plate. If another person is the offender, your mentor may be willing to run interference for you and stop the requests. Often, the best defense a mentee has is their mentor. Saying "I have discussed this with my mentor, and they feel that it's not well aligned with my current activities" or "My mentor is advising me not to take on new projects until I complete the current major project that I am working on" is one approach to respond to requests that are not aligned with your goals and priorities. If it's your mentor who's loading you with menial or unrelated work, have an open discussion about the types of things you should be doing and how to switch gears.

SUMMARY

You don't have to change who you are as a person to be a great mentee. We've seen different types of people with varying personalities, convictions, and work styles achieve their goals—and later become outstanding mentors themselves—while keeping their personal values and beliefs at the forefront.

But you should learn from those who have been immersed in mentorship for years. Adopt your mentor's good habits and practices early in your career to ensure that you put forth your best self from the start, which will also place you head and shoulders above the competition.

TAKE-HOME POINTS

- Be clear about your goals, obstacles, and projects so your mentor can give you the guidance you need.
- Perfect the art of talking less and being positive, poised, and professional in your interactions.
- Whether a small task or a major one, do what you say you will do—and do it well.
- Don't lose sight of who you are and where you are going. Check in with yourself and your mentor frequently to ensure you're headed in the direction you want to be.

Chapter 6
BEWARE THE MENTEE LANDMINES

A judicious mentee is always cognizant of being mature, responsible, and ambitious. Unfortunately, many otherwise-good mentees become too immersed in appearances, wanting to look like experts from the start. This image obsession is not only unnecessary; it can also lead to a number of perilous mistakes. We call these "mentee landmines"—and provide a path to navigate this sometimes-treacherous road.

We offer this advice because we've known too many mentees who have suffered because they succumbed to landmines—a sad fact, since many of these missteps can be avoided. In this section, we suggest ways in which to avoid the common pitfalls mentees fall prey to.

LEARN WHEN TO SAY "NO"

First and foremost, learn to say "no" politely. Being a "yes person" will not do you—or anyone else—any favors. For example, if you commit to projects that aren't relevant to your career, you'll end up burned out, which quickly spirals into low-quality work and a tarnished reputation. But how best to say "no" to things that may be low value to you? First, decide if "no" is an option; depending on your organization and your boss, it may not be. However, if you have autonomy to choose the projects on which you work, consider the "Yes-No-Yes" approach, laid out in William Ury's *The Power of a Positive No*. To illustrate, if you are asked to take a task that seems like a major time sink, ask yourself whether the assignment fits with your goals and priorities. If it doesn't, then by turning down this offer, you are saying "yes" to your goals and priorities. Second, deliver a sincere but straightforward no with an explanation: "I'm sorry, but during this critical stage in my career, I will need to focus on X (your goals and priorities), and this project doesn't fall into that category." The final aspect is saying "yes" to the relationship. You don't want to create an enemy, so it will be important to end on a pleasant and cooperative tone. For example, "Even though I am unable to assist you at this time given my looming grant deadline (insert other priorities here), please let me know if I can assist with other projects when things hopefully free up a bit more. Especially projects that are related to X, Y, or Z—I'm really trying to grow my portfolio in those areas." Additionally, you can help the person who reached out to you by referring them to others who may be able to assist with this work.

BE SELF-CONFIDENT

Mentors typically don't want to be bothered with approving or signing off on everything you do. When mentorship is built on trust, you can feel confident in moving forward with projects without the need for explicit permission from your mentor.

Ideally, you would cover this at the beginning so you know what needs your mentor's say-so and what you can do on your own. And remember that you are still learning, so there will be things you don't know. Giving answers that are incorrect or making decisions that are otherwise hasty are not likely to serve you (or your mentor) well.

ASK FOR HELP WHEN YOU NEED IT OR ARE IN DOUBT

Don't be afraid to ask for your mentor's insight or assistance when you think it is needed. After all, that's part of what a good mentor (and mentee) should do. If it's a simple question where you think you know the answer, a quick two- to three-sentence email with background and a "yes/no" reply is often all you need (as discussed in **Chapter 4**). If the issue is more complex, save it for your face-to-face meeting. Remember, your meetings are an ideal time to discuss your needs and inquiries—and an agenda that outlines this ahead of time can be invaluable.

FOCUS ON COMMUNICATION

Though it may sound cliché to say that good mentoring requires good communication, we have found this to be a universal fact. No mentorship can thrive—or even survive—without open, honest dialogue.

Master the art of positive discussions with your mentors. Learn to communicate seamlessly and clearly so that there are no doubts about what is happening, what step is next, and where you are heading. If you aren't sure of what is being recommended or what the next steps are, ask for clarification before committing or restate what was heard. Maintaining this type of "closed loop" communication helps ensure both you and your mentor are on the same wavelength and have the same expectations.

ALWAYS BE TRUTHFUL AND HONEST

Mistakes are not only part of menteeship; they are valuable opportunities for growth and reflection. Every mentor fully expects their mentees to get it wrong every now and then. When this happens (and it will), be truthful and honest. Blaming others, resenting constructive criticism, or making excuses for subpar or late work will not serve you well in the short, medium, or long term.

When you make a mistake, say so, and put in place ideas and strategies to avoid a similar incident in the future. Your honesty and willingness to admit fault will be both admirable and uncommon. Trying to fly under the radar or avoiding your mentor (so-called "ghosting") will not help. Eventually, your mentor will find out what you've been doing (or not doing), and the relationship—and your career—could quickly take a nosedive.

Remember our prior advice: if there are obstacles to moving your work forward, discuss them with your mentor at the earliest opportunity (**Chapter 5**). An effective mentor will never fault you for not making progress if they know what the barriers are. But they will fault you if you don't keep them informed.

WATCH OUT FOR MENTORSHIP MALPRACTICE

Although it's uncommon, we know of mentors who, unfortunately, assign mentees meaningless tasks or ask them to focus on projects unrelated to their interests. We call these mentors "exploiters." Exploiters value managers, not scientists or creative thinkers. They are taskmasters in that they simply want people to do the work for them. On the same spectrum are hijackers: those who take a mentee's idea without giving due credit (or, frankly, robbing them). Hijackers can come in various forms, but tales of taking first-author spots on manuscripts or submitting grants or ideas and labeling them as their own are unfortunately not rare in the scientific community.

As a mentee, you must be on the lookout for these egregious behaviors. Do not tolerate them. If you find yourself in this situation, we recommend the following: first, discuss your concerns openly with your mentor and provide them the opportunity to explain themselves. It is possible some mentors may not be aware of how this activity may hurt your growth. However, if the behavior persists, consider getting a new mentor or bringing it up with other members of your mentorship team. Being used by a mentor will not help your career and could set you up for failure.

SUMMARY

Many of the mistakes mentees make early in their careers are common and avoidable. Be on the lookout for these pitfalls—and put in place strategies to prevent or manage them. When mistakes do occur, be honest and make sure to learn from them.

TAKE-HOME POINTS

- As a mentee, you will make mistakes, but you can learn to avoid the most common—and disastrous—ones.
- Find the right balance between being confident and humble; know when to ask for help or approval.
- When you run into issues, tell your mentor. You don't want them to find out too late, which will reflect poorly on you and make the problem much more difficult to resolve.

- When mistakes do occur, embrace them as learning opportunities and make a plan to move forward.
- If your mentor is stealing your ideas or assigning you meaningless tasks, frankly discuss your concerns with them. Consider exiting the relationship if these behaviors persist.

Chapter 7
ENDING RELATIONSHIPS
WITH MENTORS

Sadly, mentorship can fail for many reasons. The worst is due to imprudent behavior from a mentor. These types of behaviors must be addressed immediately. If you let an unproductive or abusive mentorship continue, you risk career destruction.

As we briefly touched on in the previous chapter, problematic mentorship behaviors include:

- Taking credit for your ideas, underplaying work you've done for the good of the company, or substituting their name for yours. This may include not giving you the first-author position for your work, assuming full responsibility for landing a new client or customer with whom you worked, leaving your name off of a proposal or project to which you contributed substantively, or submitting a grant as the principal investigator for experiments and data that you in fact generated.
- Being possessive of their mentorship role, refusing to let others help you or work with you (we call these mentors "possessors").

- Wanting to be more of a friend than a mentor—avoiding conflict, serious discussions, or decision making (the "country clubber" mentor).
- Being unavailable because of excessive travel (the "world-traveling" mentor).
- Allowing projects to fall behind (by missing deadlines) and/or not giving you an opportunity to ask questions and discuss progress and obstacles (the "bottleneck" mentor).
- Giving you tasks or projects that won't benefit you but will make their life easier (the "exploiter").

Mentees: Do not become complicit and do not let these types of behaviors continue. You risk personal and professional demise if a mentor is being careless or malicious with their power. A bad mentor can—and should—be stopped with one or more of these strategies:

- **Establish a team of mentors.** Having others that can help address the problematic behavior can go a long way and can help you gracefully exit a bad mentorship if needed.
- **Agree upon timelines for your projects.** If your mentor is holding you up, be clear about when and why you need something from them. Tell them exactly what may happen if those deadlines aren't met (e.g., "If I don't hear from you by Friday, I'll assume you don't have any objections to my moving forward with submitting the paper"). If they let deadlines slip repeatedly, it may be time to think about a new mentor.
- **Ask others to come to your defense.** A mentorship committee can be a valuable resource to advocate for you and help you determine the benefit of projects or tasks given to you by your mentor. If unrelated or menial projects persist, bring the issue to your mentorship committee and be clear

about what types of assignments you are seeking. Normative pressure is powerful—we suspect that your mentor will be embarrassed that their mentoring malpractice behaviors will be shared with their peers. Given this, you must be careful about how this is brought up in a public setting. No one likes to be criticized in public. Feel free to discuss one-on-one with your coach (see **Chapter 2**), comentor, or supervisor to see how best to manage a wayward mentor.

- *Know when to walk away.* If all else fails, be willing and ready to call an end to the mentorship. This is not an easy task, but it's far better to quit when there is no resolution than to let a poorly matched mentorship continue. The mechanics of doing this, however, also require some planning and guidance from people who know you and your situation.

While it is impossible to provide a "one-size-fits-all" approach to these challenging and oftentimes emotionally wrenching situations, we offer three general suggestions.

First, make sure you have a place to land before ending the relationship. Ideally, you will have identified someone who has agreed to be your mentor moving forward.

Second, once you have made this decision, go forward and don't hedge, even if the original mentor promises to change. We presume that you have already had some heart-to-heart discussions and that the wayward mentor has not changed their ways so far—there is no reason to believe they will do so now. Relenting and giving them yet another chance just wastes your time and energy.

Finally, you want the relationship to end as well as possible. Remember, you chose this mentor for a reason—their success in the field, their connections, or their ability to successfully mentor others, for example. This still holds true. However, what has changed is that you have realized that the relationship is not as conducive to your success as you thought it would be. This is not the time to hurl accusations or lob personal attacks. Provided the mentor has not crossed any red lines (e.g., sexual harassment, racial discrimination, clear scientific misconduct, criminal abuse), public battles between an established mentor and a relatively unknown mentee usually don't end well for the mentee. Thus, in the absence of those issues, we recommend trying for an amicable and professional separation whenever possible. And if those issues are part of the problem, then it is important that you take the appropriate steps as directed by your organization's policies. Don't try to deal with them alone.

SUMMARY

Being a good mentee is about awareness. You need to be aware of your own professional demeanor and work ethic at all times. Similarly, you must remain aware of what you have promised and what you are delivering.

But you should also be aware of the behavior of your mentors. Allowing a mentor to take advantage of you or to abandon you without the tools you need could be disastrous. Be sure your mentorship starts out as a healthy, two-way street in which both parties understand their responsibilities. Then, reevaluate at regular intervals to ensure you're both still benefiting from the venture.

If you've chosen mentors you respect and admire (and we hope you have!), you should find that mentorship is a remarkable highlight of your learning process, shaping you into the professional you wish to become. You should also realize how hard good mentoring is to come by and think about paying it forward. Such is the lifecycle of good mentorship!

TAKE-HOME POINTS

- Mentors may engage in a variety of behaviors that spell trouble for mentees. Learn to identify these and address them immediately.
- Give yourself a "safety net" by having multiple mentors and advocates.
- When your mentor holds you up and you miss deadlines, it makes you look bad. Tell your mentor when and why you need something and what will happen if you don't hear from them within a reasonable time frame.
- Don't be afraid to end a bad mentoring relationship. It is far better to endure an awkward discussion than to allow a bad mentor to potentially ruin your career.

Chapter 8
MENTORING ACROSS GENERATIONS: FIND YOUR COMMON GROUND

We've discussed ways to choose an ideal mentee and provided strategies to get the most out of mentorship. For most, these tips will serve you well. But another factor is often overlooked: generational gaps.

It is easy to say, and think, that age and generational influences don't—or shouldn't—matter in mentorship. After all, guiding someone to be their best self should not be bound by time or cultural barriers. But the reality is that we've seen good mentoring relationships lose their momentum because of these differences.

These differences, we'd argue, are simply different roads to the same destination. But each road is shaped by a person's past experiences and upbringing, making it difficult to see that there is another way to get there—and achieve remarkable things while doing so. For the purposes of this book, at this point in time, we're talking specifically about millennials, who grew up in an environment that was markedly different from previous generations. As new generations grow up in their own environments, they will have different outlooks from the millennials—the next generation already does!

If your mentee is a millennial (born 1981–2000), your role as mentor may need to be modified in some ways to fit their styles and influences. But these would-be challenges are actually unique opportunities to accomplish great things with your millennial mentee—and to watch them flourish as you both learn how to break down generational differences and stereotypes.

Millennial mentees can certainly have the same drive and motivation as those from Generation X (1965–1980) or those who are Baby Boomers (1946–1964). But the way they work with others is often markedly different. As a result, older mentors may get frustrated or assume that their mentee doesn't respect the unwritten rules of mentorship. This can lead to miscommunication and exasperation for both parties: definitely not a recipe for successful mentorship and a rewarding learning experience.

We've seen plenty of exciting and enriching mentorships that cross age and generational boundaries. If you have the opportunity to mentor a millennial, consider the following strategies to help you both get the most out of it. But please know that we do not consider all individuals of any group to be a certain way—we are speaking as epidemiologists and making generalizations with the hope that intergenerational misunderstandings can be minimized.

ALLOW FOR SHORT AND TARGETED INTERACTIONS

It's easy to forget how much the ever-changing world molds and shapes young people who grew up in it. Thirty years ago, the Internet did not play a role at all in most workplaces. Yet today, our mentees and future workforce may not recognize a world without it.

Millennials are used to a world of information at their fingertips via smartphones and other devices. They crave instant (and succinct) communication via social media and related avenues. These tools have shaped millennials into a generation that thrives on accessibility and collaboration in a way that didn't exist when some mentors were starting their careers. This is not a bad thing. You simply need to understand their thought processes, just as they should work to understand yours.

Millennials may be more apt to send a quick email or "pop in" when they have a question as they are working through a project. They are not trying to annoy you; they are simply used to an instant and focused way of working with others. Having to wait until next week's scheduled meeting is not how they have been trained to think.

We'd argue that frequent and short touch points with millennials can be an extremely efficient way to accomplish things. So embrace the five-minute, unscheduled meeting. These "micromentoring" sessions (frequent, short, and highly targeted meetings to get something specific done) can allow your mentee to have quick check-ins with you when needed. This approach is similar to coaching, and it frees up much of your time that might otherwise be spent on longer meetings.

Today we're all used to constant interruptions by emails and text messages. If you really need some focused time without interruption, discuss this with your mentee so they are aware of when it's acceptable to interrupt—and when they will have to wait.

PUT HIERARCHY ASIDE

The traditional "subordinate role" that many mentors expect is not familiar to millennials. That doesn't mean they don't respect their superiors. Rather, millennials are used to a more open, flat structure that allows them to communicate with everyone, from the brand-new intern to the company president or department chair, without having to worry about "going through the proper channels."

It's tempting to assume the attitude of "this person should learn the proper mentee role" if they are not following what many may consider the normal protocol for talking with higher-ups in the company or department. But this is not a helpful approach for your partnership.

Chances are, your millennial mentee is simply trying to be efficient. They may think that going through two people to approach the chief financial officer or department head is a waste of other people's time, especially when they can quickly send an email directly to that person. After all, if they can get the information they need without troubling anyone else, why shouldn't they? They often also think that such acts show consideration and motivation. Remember, their generation simply isn't used to hierarchy. In an age of being able to instantly contact nearly anyone in the world via the Internet, the model is very different for these mentees. However, the hierarchy may not be so open to the "new ways," and going straight to the top person may be viewed as inappropriate by the person themselves and thus negatively impact the mentee. Teach your mentee how to navigate the hierarchy of your organization—what works, what doesn't, who is more or less approachable, how the culture works.

FOCUS ON PURPOSE, NOT PROCESS

Millennials are constantly searching for a deeper meaning - a purpose. For them, it's about the destination, not the journey. They are interested in making a difference and having an impact—on their mentor, their team, and the world around them. They care not for the details of how a mentor may think the job should be done or the series of steps they should follow. Rather, they think that they are inventive and nimble enough to figure things out on their own.

Often, they will make use of the infinite array of digital resources at their disposal to do the job better than the mentor—teaching their mentor a thing or two along the way. Other times, they may need guidance, even when they don't think that they do. It is the job of the mentor to be able to ascertain when the mentee can handle something on their own and when it is time to intervene and help prevent bad judgment or errors that may well derail the mentee's career.

What attracts and motivates millennials is whether the work they are doing will make a difference—whether it has purpose. Thus, the usual metrics used by older generations—fame, fortune, accolades, profession-specific measurements such as citation indexes—may be less relevant. Rather, millennials may respond to nontraditional values: How will this make the world a better place? Is this interesting to me? Will it make me and others happy? Mentors who can articulate a larger picture for the work at hand, how it might help humanity, or how a particular project may lead to contributions beyond academic yardsticks are thus magnetizing for millennials. At the same time, the mentor must find a way to impress upon the mentee that professional metrics, such as citations, publications, or presentations at professional events, do matter. Such metrics will impact not only their future career but also their ability to reach their larger goals. Those who can do all this—and do it well—are more likely than others to have positive relationships with millennials.

SUMMARY

It's easy to assume that the different approach that millennials take means they aren't patient, respectful, or collaborative. But for the most part, millennials (like members of every generation before and after them) want the same things you do—they just tend to go about achieving them in a different way that is a direct result of the world in which they were raised.

Millennials can teach us a lot about empowerment and engagement, as they utilize their professional network and access to instant communication for everyone's benefit. Your job, as a mentor, is to guide them to a successful career path as well as toward the virtues that cross generational lines: honesty, integrity, respect, and hard work.

TAKE-HOME POINTS

- Younger generations are our future workforce—and they need mentors to help them find success and, ultimately, drive progress in their field.
- Millennials thrive on frequent and short interactions that help them keep their projects moving. Embrace this and forget about traditional long meetings if they don't fit your mentee's goals and pace. When new generations begin to fill the ranks of up-and-coming physicians, adjust your mentoring style accordingly.
- A mentee who approaches someone on an upper level isn't being insubordinate; they are likely just trying to be efficient and considerate. Or they may be trying to do an end-around. Learn how to tell the difference.
- Consider whether you and your millennial mentee can benefit from a nontraditional mentorship that is fast, focused, and driven by a specific project or goal.
- Remember that millennials savor purpose over process. Focus on the big picture whenever possible, but don't always skip the details—they may be crucial to your mentee's success. Knowing which approach to use, and when, is essential to mentoring across generations.

Chapter 9
MENTORING ACROSS DIVERSITY WITH A FOCUS ON WOMEN

When you think about your prospective mentee, what image comes to mind? Do you picture someone like yourself, with a similar cultural background and ethnicity? Or do you envision someone with a particular aptitude, background, training, and pedigree?

In the process of writing this book, we had a very serious discussion about how to discuss mentoring across diversity. What was clear was that the issue of diversity was important enough to justify its own chapter. Why? Beyond promoting equity, a diverse team or workforce is key to maximizing innovative and remarkable contributions to any field. Diverse teams—and we define diversity broadly—provide varied views that ultimately benefit you, your organization, and your industry as a whole. When any particular group is not given a fair shot at opportunities, entire fields miss out on the enormous potential of a workforce that comes from varied walks of life with different knowledge and perspectives. Mentorship is a key element in promoting and ensuring diversity today and for the future. Hence, not including this topic would be a disservice to mentorship.

We also recognize, however, that while many issues faced by underrepresented groups are similar, they are also distinct. Entire chapters, or even books, could be dedicated to discussing mentorship for each group. Rather than generalize across all types of diversity, or risk oversimplifying a complex issue, we decided to provide an in-depth discussion of mentorship for one particular group that has struggled for equity: women. Ideally, some of the lessons we discuss in this chapter can apply to other situations as well.

Why women? We've already alluded to some of the difficulties faced by women—particularly related to mentorship. Women are much less likely to be mentored or sponsored. This deficit likely plays a role in the continued pay, promotion, and leadership gap faced by women in the workforce. And because there are few women currently in leadership roles, it often falls upon men to mentor women. Yet men (especially after the #MeToo and Time's Up movements) are often hesitant to mentor—or be alone with—women. Fortunately, through campaigns like #HeForShe, many men have taken note and started to participate in the dialogue.

Beyond the moral arguments for diversity and gender equity, mentoring across diversity can be great for academia or any organization. Diversity opens up communications and can improve creativity. Organizations become more profitable. And mentees who were otherwise disenfranchised will learn what it takes to be successful, opening up doors for themselves and their own mentees to succeed. Importantly, not all of our suggestions will apply to everyone as culture strongly influences gender and gender norms. Open communication without assumptions or biases is always the best rule. However, within these limitations, we suggest several recommendations to help ensure that all mentees receive the high-quality mentoring they deserve.

FOR MENTORS

1. Take Stock of Your Mentoring Activities

The first step toward mentoring women is to be cognizant of giving equal opportunities to everyone. This means mentoring, sponsoring, coaching, and building connections for people regardless of their gender, how they look, what they believe, and where they are from. Even small things, like tweeting, referencing, and calling out people for their accomplishments, can be righted by mentors. Language is important—use the same terms for everyone. For example, women are often called "hardworking" and "caring" while men are called "knowledgeable," "ambitious," or "skilled." Be mindful of your own practice and personal biases and try to distribute your time, energy, and accolades as equitably as possible.

It's also important to know that some individuals may not seek out mentorship as aggressively as others do. For instance, studies have shown that women are less likely to ask for mentorship or sponsorship than their male counterparts. This means it may be up to the mentor to keep a keen eye out for undiscovered talent. Having mentored many women in our careers, we can tell you unequivocally that you should do it! It's worth it—and has enriched our careers tremendously.

2. Behave Professionally

When you are with your mentee, we recommend that you behave as if others are watching the interaction. This doesn't mean, for example, that you need to leave a door open when alone with a woman mentee, but it does mean that you should keep your language and your actions professional. You don't need to behave differently either. Rather, be professional regardless of whom you are with. Model good behavior and integrity. The people you mentor are learning what you say, how you say it, and how you act all the time. If you behave unprofessionally in private, so will they. Consider this: would you want the comment you just made broadcast on the evening news? Or read by your partner? If not—rethink it. Furthermore, try not to speak in gender (or other) stereotypes (e.g., women are emotional, men have more leadership potential). Make this a habit, and others around you will start to follow your lead. People who may not have approached you to be a mentee may even begin to come to you for advice and mentorship.

One important piece of advice: do not comment on physical appearance. Women especially (but various ethnic groups as well) are often judged by their appearances. The language you use will be rife with unintended meaning, even if you don't mean it to be.

Finally, as the person with more power, don't initiate physical contact. If you feel comfortable, you can return a hug/handshake/high five that is offered. Otherwise, remember that every person has a different level of comfort with physical touch. You don't know where theirs is. If you initiate, they may feel the need to acquiesce to physical contact because of the power differential. And that creates discomfort, which may attenuate your effectiveness as a mentor.

3. One Size Does Not Fit All

Just because your mentee is a woman, don't assume that they . . . anything. Children. Family. Work-life balance. Don't make assumptions. This is particularly true for pregnant (or recently pregnant) women who have a high risk of experiencing bias and discrimination. Think a mentee won't want to travel or work evenings because they just had a baby? Ask them. It may be true. But it also may not. Everyone does not have the same priorities and goals, so avoid making assumptions. Communication here is key. Don't exclude your mentee from opportunities because you assume they are not interested.

4. Don't Cut off Anyone from Networking Opportunities

One-on-one experiences can often enhance mentoring relationships and bonding. Be smart about it. Consider a cup of coffee instead of alcohol. Meet in a public place at work rather than off-site. If you do decide to have a drink, make sure intoxication is not possible by either party (this is true regardless of who your mentees are). Distinguish private, social activities (for example, a golf outing that only includes men) from professional mentorship events. If certain mentees are not invited to participate in a professional mentorship event based on their gender (or other characteristics), that is bad mentorship.

5. Avoid Acting Out Gender Scripts

Gender scripts refers to social norms that relate to particular identities, behaviors, and relationships. For example, a male mentor may unconsciously activate a gender script and limit a female mentee's autonomy. Be mindful of when this may be affecting the way you are treating your mentee. Are you rescuing them? Instead, try to facilitate them rescuing themselves. By doing so, you help them gain skills they can use in the future and allow them to stretch to their full potential.

Relatedly, thanks to cultural expectations, women often feel more comfortable expressing emotions than men do. This does not mean they're "emotional" or "unstable." This means they're passionate and committed. Though this may mean you see more tears with women mentees, it also means they may be better able to pick up and address unspoken dynamics in a room. This skill could make them better at building consensus, networking, and heading off problems. So instead of recoiling, become comfortable with emotions. This will benefit both you and your mentee.

FOR MENTEES

1. Make Sure to Have a Mentorship Team

We've already emphasized the importance of having more than one mentor. But having a mentorship team can be especially beneficial for women. The mentee is generally the most affected if a mentorship relationship sours. Having mentors to turn to can help protect you from the consequences of having to sever one key relationship (especially if it must be done quickly). This team can also provide emotional and political support if mentors misbehave.

Another consideration is adding a woman to your mentorship team. It may be difficult to find a woman specifically in your area (given lower numbers of women in leadership). However, having a senior woman as a mentor (or coach) can be helpful when discussing issues you may not feel comfortable discussing more broadly.

2. Become Comfortable with Conflict

Women are often socialized to be agreeable. Being courteous is beneficial; being compliant can be detrimental in the workplace, where honesty and directness are appreciated. For example, as discussed in **Chapter 6**, it is important to learn to say "no" to projects that do not align well with your goals and your other professional activities.

Likewise, letting a minor disagreement fester does everyone harm and destroys trust. To be clear, we are not recommending for you to be argumentative. However, it is important to become comfortable expressing disagreement in a direct and constructive manner—especially with your mentor. As with many things, practice makes perfect. Practice calmly disagreeing (always focusing on the facts, never on the person) in front of the mirror or with a friend. Try using William Ury's "Yes-No-Yes" approach (as discussed in **Chapter 6**). Force yourself to commit to a difficult discussion by putting the topic on your mentorship meeting agenda. The more you practice speaking up and approaching conflict in a healthy way, the more comfortable you'll become.

3. Be Professional

In a perfect world, we would not be judged by our outward appearance. Remember that humans make initial judgments about who you are and how capable you are within seconds of meeting you. With this judgment comes stereotypes—especially for women. Although we do not advocate for the suppression of personal style or dressing counter to your personal or religious beliefs, a professional appearance for your work environment is a good idea. Dress for success. Dress a notch above your current level (what are the bosses wearing?). Don't let what you wear be the limiting factor for who you aspire to be. Rather, dress the role so that you immediately project where you want to be.

4. Fake It 'til You Make It, Then Realize You're Not Faking It

Confidence is a highly regarded quality among leaders. After all, it is difficult to follow someone who is unsure or hesitant. Even though confidence does not necessarily mean competence, it falls to logic that if you are competent, you will become more accomplished, and once you become more accomplished, you can begin to feel more confident. Unfortunately, this logic does not always translate well for individuals who may suffer from the "imposter syndrome." The imposter syndrome occurs when successful people are unconvinced of their abilities and fear being discovered as imposters, undeserving to be in their current position.

Although anyone can suffer from the imposter syndrome (and typically everyone does at some point in their life), women, minorities, and "first-generation" employees (those who are first in their family to do the job) have higher—and more persistent—rates of imposter syndrome. Women may have experienced a lifetime of people (even strangers) doubting their abilities, role, or leadership position based on their gender alone.

Unfortunately, lacking confidence as a mentee can lead you to becoming too dependent on your mentor's support and advice. This can become draining and time-consuming for the mentor. Avoid this situation by developing a plan to deal with problems that may come up. Consult with your peers on low-level problems that don't require your mentor's advice. Early on, though, you may have to fake it to make it. Act with confidence. This helps alleviate anxiety before talks, important negotiations, or meetings with a superior. You should remember that while you may not know everything, you are where you are because you are competent, have been successful, and will continue to be. Consider developing a personal mantra that you can recite to yourself during times of doubt. Some examples are "I am enough," "I can do anything," and "This too shall pass."

5. Seek Out Peers

Successful women often recall the importance of having colleagues at approximately their level in the organization to talk to about issues as they arise and to provide much-needed support as they ascend the professional ladder together. Such individuals go by different names depending on the organization or context but can be referred to as "peer mentors" or "peer advisors."

While such peers are traditionally not part of your formal mentorship team (and certainly do not replace formal mentorship by senior individuals), having people you can relate to as members of your mentoring ecosystem can help in many ways. First, it can validate your experiences. You may find yourself asking, "Am I overreacting? Was that comment really inappropriate?" Second, having a group of nonjudgmental peers who are at your level or have experienced similar realities can help you strategize and problem-solve. For example, there may be issues you don't feel comfortable discussing with your traditional mentors. But collectively, your peers may have shared those problems. Use their experiences to help you manage yours. This is especially important if you experience harassment or bias—peers can help by calling it as such. In addition, peers can provide an infusion of confidence and support. Women often won't apply for jobs unless they meet every single job requirement, while men often apply when they meet only some, and not all, of the posted requirements. Having a peer group to support you in "reach" or "stretch" decisions is helpful, as it often turns out that they weren't reaches at all. Finally, having a supportive peer group may improve connectivity, reduce burnout, and make life as a mentee more pleasant. But it is important that a mentee feels comfortable interacting in such a setting. Not all cultures advocate this type of interaction, and it is important to be mindful of that.

SUMMARY

Though it may be tempting to avoid potential pitfalls by not mentoring women (or individuals with whom we may not readily identify), it is critical that mentors step up to mentor young professionals across gender, race, socioeconomic, cultural, political, and religious groups. By modeling good behavior, mentors can help create an environment that embraces diversity and inclusion, strives for excellence and professional success, and improves the well-being of organizations as a whole. Doing so, above all else, requires professionalism. Mentors and mentees can also help by being mindful of each other's personal and cultural differences and of their own habits and biases.

TAKE-HOME POINTS

- Effective mentorship will help promote diversity.
- Both mentors and mentees should strive to behave professionally and with integrity at all times.
- Mentors should be mindful to mentor, sponsor, coach, and connect mentees equitably, regardless of gender, race, ethnicity, religious beliefs, sexual orientation, political views, social class, cultural upbringing, country of origin, or any other factor that makes us who we are.
- Be mindful of biases. Make sure not to make assumptions about mentees (or mentors) or act out gender scripts. Instead, open communication is key.
- Don't exclude women—or any individual—from mentoring, networking opportunities, or social events.
- Mentees should become comfortable with conflict and have a strategy to combat self-doubt when it arises.
- Mentees should ensure they have a diverse mentoring team; women may find it helpful to seek out a supportive peer network and include women on their mentorship team.

Chapter 10
LOOKING BACK WHILE
TRAVELING FORWARD

We thought it important to close with some parting words of wisdom by looking back on how best to operationalize the advice in these pages and by looking forward to what is on the horizon that mentors and mentees should be aware of.

LOOKING BACK

We know that first-time mentors or mentees may feel anxious or uneasy about the responsibility of mentorship and its importance both in their professional careers and in their field in general. In addition, mentoring someone of a different gender, race, age group, or background can take many people into unfamiliar territory. Mentors, especially those who are newly in a position to help others, may place unnecessary burdens on themselves to ensure that their first experience is successful. Similarly, a brand-new employee or a junior faculty member in search of a mentor at a new institution

71

may be too paralyzed by anxiety to actively seek out the help that will be crucial to their success in the field.

These perceived barriers can often prevent people from seeking a mentor or serving as one. In the academic world as well as in many corporate organizations, this can be the kiss of death.

For us, receiving the help of a mentor and then serving in this role to help others has been career transforming. Such experiences have enriched our lives and our views of the world. In fact, we can point with gratitude to our individual mentors for guiding us to our current positions. We have also experienced the sheer delight that comes when your mentee has made it—been recognized for their abilities and talents—and assumes positions of influence. We continue to appreciate learning about the challenges our mentees face—many of which are different than the ones we faced, whether related to professional conflicts, balancing work with life, or confronting mentors that treat mentees unfairly.

We hear from colleagues outside of academia that this same appreciation—respect, even—for the mentoring relationship holds true in other industries and fields. For example, when top CEOs are asked what the keys to their success are, a good mentor or guide is commonly acknowledged.

Put simply, mentorship is too valuable an opportunity to let slip by because of uncertainty or anxiety regarding the outcome. But we are also realists. We know that not just anyone can be a good mentor right from the start—it takes practice, patience, trial and error. And we know that there are experienced and successful people in any field whose personalities, priorities, or dispositions preclude them from being an effective mentor to most mentees. But we believe those people are the exceptions. And we trust that your reading this book is a signal that, within you, lies the patience and commitment to learn to become an effective mentor.

LOOKING FORWARD

While much has been written about mentorship—we have annotated the key articles and books that have been produced on this topic in the **Appendix**—we believe that there will be an even greater focus on this topic in the years ahead.

The reasons are severalfold. First, the various roles that a more experienced person can have in helping a more junior person—traditional mentor, coach, sponsor, connector—have only recently been clearly identified and delineated. We expect there will be even more studies and publications about these diverse types of "mentors"—and how each contributes to a mentee's success. Just like we now have suggestions for what makes a good mentor, we will also likely have guidance on what makes a good coach or an effective sponsor.

Second, people just starting in a field are now generally more actively engaged in finding and securing a mentor. Relatedly, institutions, organizations, and companies are increasingly formalizing such mentoring relationships by proactively forming mentoring teams or constituting "launch" committees. Many organizations have workforce development (or, in universities, faculty development) leads whose jobs are to ensure that mentees receive the help they need to succeed.

Finally, the heightened focus on diversity, equity, and inclusion has led organizations to pay more attention to the needs of underrepresented groups through special workshops and seminars focusing on the unique challenges many such employees face. An example is the "Executive Leadership Course in Academic Medicine"—started in 1995 by Drexel University—that is open to only female faculty at academic medical centers. Another example is the National Research Mentoring Network, funded by the National

Institutes of Health, which trains mentors in "Culturally Aware Mentorship" to promote the success of researchers who come from historically underrepresented backgrounds. Harvard's South Asian Healthcare Leaders Forum (SAHLF—with which we are proud to partner) is another example of a specific organization aimed at creating and mentoring future healthcare leaders from Southeast Asia.

So, what is on the horizon? We predict there will be an increasing number of workshops, seminars, and teaching sessions on how to become better at mentoring and how to be a more successful mentee. Indeed, "mentoring academies" will likely be held in various academic centers around the United States. Just as the number of professional coaches has skyrocketed over the past few years (newly minted senior executives now often ask to have such an individual to guide them when they are negotiating their job package), we expect there will be an increase in those who are employed to help match mentors with mentees and ensure that those relationships blossom.

One important component that remains a work in progress is regular evaluations and assessments of how well an organization is suited to foster and promote mentoring activities within its walls. For example, we are familiar with culture-of-safety questionnaires that have been used for over a decade in US hospitals to identify how healthcare workers feel about the commitment level of their leaders and colleagues to ensuring patient safety. It has also been used to intervene and make changes at the hospital-unit level such as improving communication between nurses and physicians or bettering alignment between senior executives and frontline workers. In this spirit, we believe that the time is right for more widespread use of organizational mentoring climate surveys that provide a snapshot of how employees feel about the mentoring that goes on (or doesn't) at their institution. The data generated from such a survey—which can be analyzed at the overall level or at a more granular unit level—can be used to pinpoint problems, highlight possible deficiencies, and structure interventions. Such a tool could also be used to help attract mentors and mentees to institutions that score high on such assessments. We have included references to two such tools in the references section of this chapter.

We know our approach in this book has been US-centric. This is not surprising given that is where we have been mentoring for most of our adult lives (even though two of us were born in the developing world). We believe that the United States has a more robust approach to mentoring than most other countries, including advanced economic nations such as Japan, Australia, India, Italy, and England. This is certainly true for academic medical centers in these countries (which we have been privileged to see firsthand). Thus, much of the future interest in mentoring may reside internationally, since workforce development and career success for young people is every bit as important in those nations as it is in the United States.

It is an exciting time to be interested in mentoring. We look forward to both watching and helping to shape the future of this important field.

FINAL THOUGHTS

We urge you to put hesitation aside and consider a mentorship opportunity because effective and mutually beneficial mentoring relationships are fundamental to career success in every field. We hope the practical guidance provided in this book helps alleviate any fears you may have.

Mentors: You have the chance to provide real-world experience to new and upcoming members of your area of study while learning more about yourself and your own personal strengths.

Mentees: The right mentor is a virtual gold mine of learning experience that cannot be found in a textbook, YouTube video, or TED Talk.

We encourage both mentors and mentees to focus on the potentially transformative experience that could lie ahead with a successful mentoring relationship. With careful planning and effective communication, well-matched mentors and mentees are poised for a memorable and enjoyable adventure that solidifies further success within their field.

Successful mentorship does more than provide benefits for the involved parties: it paves the way for further achievement, breakthrough, and knowledge for generations to come. We hope this book will illuminate your path. It is a future we look forward to seeing.

APPENDIX
Annotated References and Further Reading

Altman I. The Dos and Don'ts of Mentoring. Forbes. 2017.

This article presents three broad tips for both mentors and mentees.

1. ***Create structure.*** Know how, when, and for how long a given mentoring relationship will last. Define the parameters of the relationship—from meeting times and locations to long-term goals—and know what it will encompass from the beginning.

2. ***Don't be the hero.*** Mentors must let mentees make mistakes if they want them to grow. If the mentor completely protects the mentee from mistakes, there is no chance for learning and growth. Therefore, the mentor should guide, correcting course when mistakes happen and reinforcing good behaviors and outcomes.

3. ***Be coachable.*** Mentors cannot dispense all the answers, and mentees must be able to take what direction they are given—and have the right attitude to benefit from what the mentor has to offer.

Blackman A. Misguided Guidance: 12 Mistakes Mentors Should Avoid. Modern Workforce: Everwise. 2014.

This quick-hits article puts together a list of 12 mistakes mentors make.

1. ***Unsolicited advice.*** Giving advice on something outside the scope of the particular mentor-mentee dyad. Focus on the defined goals of the relationship.
2. ***Being too harsh.*** Criticism is good in moderation. Too much can damage the relationship.
3. ***Being impatient.*** Guide the mentee to their destination—do not push them there.
4. ***Trying to make them into you.*** Do not try to clone yourself onto your mentee. Their path will likely be different from yours.
5. ***Lack of preparation.*** The time commitment for mentoring goes beyond meeting with your mentee. Prepare in advance and reflect after meetings to maximize your potential impact.
6. ***Narrow focus on problems.*** Some problems can stem from broader problems or tendencies that should be addressed.
7. ***Hiding your missteps.*** Because mentors are both role models and guides, there can be a conflict between the priorities of those two positions. Instead of trying to appear as the perfect role model, share your mistakes and failures when relevant. That can be just as valuable to your mentee.
8. ***Assumptions.*** There is typically a large gap in experience between mentors and mentees, but at times mentors can forget just how much their mentee has yet to learn.
9. ***Mentoring the wrong person.*** Not every mentor is the right fit for every mentee—and vice versa. Try to match

skills and personalities, but if it isn't going to work out, help your mentee find a more suitable mentor.

10. **Dependency.** A critical aspect of mentoring is putting your mentee in a position to develop and trust their own judgment. Don't allow the mentee to remain dependent on your experience for too long.

11. **Telling too many stories.** Personal anecdotes can be a powerful means to make a point, but try not to get overly self-indulgent.

12. **Trying to eliminate every mistake.** While it is certainly incumbent upon you as the mentor to help your mentee avoid career-damaging mistakes, not all errors are equal. Allow the mentee to build resilience by weathering a few problems on their own.

Byerley JS. Mentoring in the Era of #MeToo. JAMA. 2018; 319:1199-200.

In light of the recent surge of very public revelations of sexual harassment and abuse, this article takes on the sensitive topic of mentoring between women and men in today's environment. The author relates the ways in which her male mentors have ensured that she feels comfortable to work with them:

- Demonstrating exemplary professional behavior, free of inappropriate or flirtatious interactions
- Always behaving as if someone else is watching, which is one way of demonstrating integrity
- Refraining from physical touch except when most anyone would find it perfectly appropriate
- Avoiding comments about appearance or making broad, generalized comments about gender

Beyond these basics of decency, though, the author points out one of the most important ways male mentors can help their female mentees: speaking up when other men do not (or worse, offend) and sponsoring women into leadership roles.

Cho CS, Ramanan RA, Feldman MD. Defining the Ideal Qualities of Mentorship: A Qualitative Analysis of the Characteristics of Outstanding Mentors. Am J Med. 2011;124:453–8.

This study sought to identify the important qualities of outstanding mentors by qualitatively analyzing the letters written by the mentees who nominated them for prestigious mentoring awards. The authors analyzed 53 letters, concluding that highly regarded mentors shared the following traits:

- Admirable personal qualities (enthusiasm, compassion, selflessness)
- Offered individualized guidance
- Devoted considerable and regular time to mentoring each of their mentees
- Supported a good personal and professional life balance
- Set an example for their mentees to later become mentors themselves

Chopra V, Arora VM, Saint S. Will You Be My Mentor? Four Archetypes to Help Mentees Succeed in Academic Medicine. JAMA Intern Med. 2018;178:175–6.

When most people think about a mentor-mentee dyad, they think of the "traditional mentor," who typically provides a longitudinal, long-lasting relationship focused on the mentee's overall career development. In addition to this form of mentorship, though, this article describes three more archetypes for mentoring:

1. **The Coach.** Task- or problem-specific advice and guidance given to assist the mentee with a specific issue or problem.
2. **The Sponsor.** Provides visibility to the mentee, a "leg up" on the ladder of their careers.
3. **The Connector.** This is typically a senior leader with extensive social and political capital that they expend to promote the legacy of the field as a whole.

There are, therefore, several types of mentorship—not all of which require the same skills or type of commitment that the traditional mentor position requires.

Chopra V, Dixon-Woods M, Saint S. The Four Golden Rules of Effective Menteeship. BMJ Careers. 2016.

While the volume of text written about mentorship is rather large, comparatively little has been written about menteeship. Through author reflection as well as reaching out to other MD or PhD mentors, this article puts together four key best practices for the mentee to adopt.

Mentees should select the right mentors to form a mentorship team, since it's rare anymore to find a single mentor who can guide a mentee in all aspects of their career. Because there is no simple way to identify good mentor matches, mentees need to remain vigilant against "mentorship malpractice"—mentor activities that can harm a mentee's career.

The mentee must be mindful of the limited time and attention a mentor has for them. Utilizing the concept of "managing up" from business, the mentee should propose options for the mentor to consider for any given topic.

As with any important relationship, communicating well is vitally important to the success of the dyad. Beginning the relationship with a clear understanding of the mentee's goals and expectations will help focus efforts on both sides. The mentee should provide timely updates to the mentor on upcoming or ongoing projects or correspondence with others (such as journals or funding agencies). Finally, planning ahead when mentor input is needed is critical. Frequent last-minute pleas for help are unlikely to be well received.

Lastly, the mentee should endeavor to be a consummate professional: committed to the work, positive in their approach, and willing to take advice and feedback in a constructive manner. Not only will these qualities contribute to a positive dynamic in the dyad; they will quickly help prove the mentee as a valuable contributor to the broader institutional and scientific community.

Chopra V, Edelson DP, Saint S. Mentorship Malpractice. JAMA. 2016;315:1453–4.

The negative behaviors of mentors can be broken down into six categories, divided into active and passive malpractice.

- Active Malpractice
  1. **The Hijacker.** By far the worst—is interested only in whatever they can take from the mentee. For the mentee, there is no defense against this form of malpractice, and once the behavior is identified, a quick and complete exit is the only option.
  2. **The Exploiter.** Self-serving in another way, this kind of bad actor pawns off low-yield activities on the mentee in the guise of learning experiences. This type of malpractice is seen in mentors who value mentees not for their scientific ideas but as managers for their own projects. While it is possible to counteract this type of malpractice, if the mentee cannot limit the behavior through firm

boundaries or additional mentors, it's time for them to
exit the relationship.

3. **The Possessor.** Fundamentally insecure in their own
abilities, they will not share responsibility of a mentee
with others. When a mentee encounters such a mentor,
they must insist on a mentorship committee if they want
to continue to work with this person.

- Passive Malpractice

    1. **The Bottleneck.** This type of mentor is simply too busy
    be an effective mentor, but agrees to be one regardless.
    This leads to delays in working with the mentee or missed
    deadlines, both of which can negatively impact the men-
    tee's career. Firm deadlines—and clear communication
    about the impact of missing them—must be set and
    enforced for the mentee to work with this kind of mentor.

    2. **The Country Clubber.** These types cannot abide con-
    flict in any form. As such, they will not advocate for the
    mentee—for resources or protected time, for example. The
    mentee's response should be to ensure they have a men-
    torship team that includes someone who will advocate
    for them.

    3. **The World Traveler.** This type of mentor is typically so
    accomplished in their own career that they are in high
    demand for things like speaking engagements and, as
    such, jet off to destination after world destination. Their
    motivation is typically their own academic success and
    personal ambitions, but the primary impact to the men-
    tee is limited face-to-face interaction to move projects
    forward. The key for the mentee is to establish regular
    times and modes of communication, often setting things
    up well in advance.

The mentee needs to look out for all of these archetypes, but the keys to combating these forms of mentorship malpractice can be summed up as follows: don't be complicit, set boundaries and communicate needs, establish a mentorship team, and know when to walk away.

Chopra V, Saint S. 6 Things Every Mentor Should Do. Harv Bus Rev. 2017.

The authors provide a concise list of keys to being a successful mentor.

- **Choose mentees carefully.** Mentoring is a commitment of the mentor's time and energy, so it is important to choose a good and compatible mentee on whom to expend those resources. Early on, when evaluating a potential new mentee, a mentor can try setting a task that will allow the mentor to evaluate the mentee's commitment and work style to ensure it is a good match for the mentor.
- **Establish a mentorship team.** Due to how busy everyone is these days, plus the fact that people tend not to stay on a single project or even at a single institution for their entire careers anymore, a team of mentors is quickly becoming the new normal for mentorship. The primary mentor is the go-to, the one responsible for the bulk of the support for the mentee, but the team should be filled out with content and subject matter experts who work well with each other as well as the mentee.
- **Run a tight ship.** Start the mentorship with a clear understanding of your commitments and the mentee's expectations for the relationship. Resolve any ambiguity early, lest it prove costly later. Develop and stick to schedules of communication and levels of quality, or be prepared for both of your careers to suffer. In the end, ensure that the mentee

understands that they are your student and should be open to and accepting of constructive criticism.

- **Head off rifts—or resolve them.** A responsibility of the mentor is to try to predict conflicts so they never happen at all (if possible), but if not, resolving them still lies with the mentor. Proactive approaches to problematic issues must be taken, and openness and honesty should go both directions. That way, many issues can be avoided altogether, but even when they come up, it is possible to repair the rift rather than letting the mentorship fizzle.

- **Don't commit mentorship malpractice.** Suffice it to say, never intentionally seek to harm the career of your mentee. Some behaviors may sneak in unnoticed, though. Be sure to evaluate your own behavior to seek out and stop these: taking credit from your mentee; insisting that mentees advance your projects over theirs; handcuffing a mentee to your timeline; attempting to prevent your mentee from working with other mentors; and/or allowing your mentee to repeat self-destructive mistakes—"mentee missteps."

- **Prepare for the transition.** Ultimately—beyond the individual success of your mentee—the hope is that they will go on to become a mentor as well. Help prepare your mentee for this transition by actively discussing it and preparing for that time.

Clark D. Your Career Needs Many Mentors, Not Just One. Harv Bus Rev. 2017.

Rather than the traditional single-mentor model, this article supports the idea of a "mentor board of directors." While less formal than a mentorship team, this idea may prove more operationalizable for many people. The author encourages mentees to seek respectable mentors who have the experience and knowledge that are pertinent to their career path, regardless of age and job title. In order to pick out the right mentors, a mentee must first perform a thorough self-examination, deciding where their career should go and, by extension, what skills and knowledge they need to accomplish that. Once they have these identified, the next step is to identify the people in their network from whom they might be able to gain key skills and experiences. Given that the people on the list may be widely scattered across the country or even the world, finding ways to make time to work with them may prove challenging. Through some creative (often informal) means, it is usually possible to make this work to the mentees' benefit. It is particularly important (as with many relationships) that the mentees make themselves valuable to their mentors in return. The nature of that reciprocation will vary, of course, depending on the skills the mentee has and what might be appropriate to offer to the mentor.

DeCastro R, Sambuco D, Ubel PA, Stewart A, Jagsi R. Mentor Networks in Academic Medicine: Moving beyond a Dyadic Conception of Mentoring for Junior Faculty Researchers. Acad Med. 2013;88.

Formal establishment of a mentoring relationship is often a requirement for career development award programs like those funded by the National Institutes of Health. Even so, a full understanding of the perspectives from people who receive these awards on mentoring has not been well studied. This qualitative study found three central ideas common to mentors and mentees alike in academic medicine:

1. There are numerous roles a mentor might play.
2. A single mentor is unlikely to be able to fulfill the diverse mentoring needs of an individual.

3. In order to address both of these issues, mentoring "networks" should be established to fulfill the mentoring needs of a mentee.

The traditional hierarchical mentor dyad no longer seems to work in academic medicine, and mentees are encouraged to develop, maintain, and evolve mentor networks. These networks should be composed of mentors who reflect the particular needs of a given mentee while attempting to maintain a diverse collection of expertise, seniority, and gender.

Farnell R. Mentor People Who Aren't Like You. Harv Bus Rev. 2017.

Humans naturally better identify with people who are more similar to themselves rather than those that are different. These underlying biases are a particular problem for mentors. Without a conscious effort to combat them, mentors would likely choose people in whom they see themselves, which would tend to concentrate the benefits of mentorship into a homogenous group. Those who are members of any particular minority group may find it hard to speak up to advance their careers, as a member of the majority group may not understand where they are coming from. Without a concerted effort to address all team members' concerns, some may go unheard.

Mentors must "close the gap," as the author states, to ensure that the needs of those who may not feel comfortable speaking up are addressed. More than a commitment to a diverse team, though, mentoring those unlike oneself has direct benefits to the mentor as well. It broadens one's understanding of other points of view, which can deepen a sense of empathy toward those who may not look like, speak like, or have the same belief systems as ourselves.

Gallo A. Demystifying Mentoring. Harv Bus Rev. 2011.

The mentorship idea itself has evolved, though many people still cling to what mentoring was in the past. Four myths are addressed in an effort to help mentees understand what they may need to do in today's fast-paced and changeable jobs. The common **myths** are:

1. ***You have to find one perfect mentor.*** The idea of having to seek out and select the perfect mentor—the one the mentee will always work with—has become a thing of the past. Careers are too dynamic these days to expect that to work. The response to this myth is that networks of people should be leveraged to gain similar (if not better) benefits as the static dyad of the past provided.

2. ***Mentoring is a formal long-term relationship.*** The need to establish and formally define a given relationship as a "mentoring relationship" may not fit with the fast-paced job and career paths people typically have these days. Mentoring can occur in one-off, short interactions or can be as casual as identifying one person a mentee goes to for advice on a particular topic. In fact, use of the title "mentor" for these types of interactions should be avoided, the author suggests.

3. ***Mentoring is for junior people.*** No matter the point of one's career, there are typically opportunities for mentoring. The traditional idea of a mentee seeking out a mentor early in their career still holds true, but it is merely the beginning, not the goal, of mentoring. Transition points are much more common now in people's careers, and those are particularly good times to seek out mentoring or advice from people who have experience and are willing to share.

4. ***Mentoring is something more experienced people do out of the goodness of their hearts.*** As with any relationship, mentoring is about give-and-take, and balancing what each party can provide to the other for mutual benefit. While there is a degree of honor in being asked to mentor, they should still get something back from the mentee. That needn't be a "direct barter," as the author states, but even the promise of assistance in the future may make it worthwhile to the mentor to help out.

The article closes with several detailed case studies in mentoring and transitions, which are well worth the read.

Gladwell M. The Tipping Point: How Little Things Can Make a Big Difference. Boston, MA: Little, Brown; 2006.

Trends, behaviors, and ideas in society often begin with a single contagious behavior that gradually reaches its critical mass, or tipping point, says Gladwell. It then tips over the threshold and spreads like wildfire. Just one person or group of people who have the right characteristics can spread major societal influences with the right conditions. In the way that a flu epidemic starts with one person, so too can social trends, crime rates, or bestselling books explode across a society from small and seemingly under-the-radar beginnings.

Gladwell illustrates such an idea with a fashion trend. A handful of young people started wearing Hush Puppy shoes, which were on the brink of extinction, to clubs in downtown Manhattan in the mid-1990s. Others noticed the shoes and the wearers, sought them out at the stores, and began wearing them. The cycle continued until the Hush Puppy trend reached its tipping point, which led to a revival of the shoe style and an all-time sales record for the company. All the while, the only "marketing" for the idea was carried out by those few who instigated the trend at the Manhattan clubs.

Those young people possessed a specific and exceptional set of social gifts, which the author calls the "Law of the Few." The Law of the Few depends heavily on the nature of the messenger. The messenger must fit into one or more of these categories: the "Connector," the "Maven," and the "Salesman."

A Connector knows a lot of people—usually far more than the average person—and is a common denominator between people who might not otherwise meet. Connectors don't stick to one "type" of acquaintance; rather, they get to know people across social, economic, and professional barriers. Connectors don't have to work hard to know so many people; they have a natural ability to relate to people in different circles through their energy, confidence, and natural ability to make friends.

Mavens, who are equally necessary to the Law of the Few, are people who soak up knowledge like a sponge and have an ability and strong desire to share it with others. They are not know-it-alls but rather want to help others solve problems with what they know. Mavens often accomplish this with the help of their natural curiosity and strong desire to learn, coupled with intelligence and spirit. They are experts—and well-known and respected as such.

The Salesman is someone who has a gift of natural persuasion. This is the third and final personality type Gladwell outlines in the Law of the Few. The Salesman uses charisma and subtle conversational skills to encourage people to go along with their ideas rather than strong-arming people to agree with them. They often possess a magnetic personality that draws people into their influences naturally, without force.

It's not just the messenger but the content of the message that allows something to reach the "Tipping Point," argues Gladwell. The

"Stickiness Factor" is what makes the message memorable and effective. To be sticky, the message must have a personal and practical quality for the recipient and must be packaged in a way that the recipient absorbs it and moves toward action because of it.

And finally, the Power of Context is the condition and circumstances of the times and places in which messages occur. These environmental factors have an equally crucial impact on the Tipping Point. Humans are deeply sensitive to the context in which something is communicated, Gladwell says.

While certain problems and obstacles may seem, at first glance, to be immovable, they can be changed or overcome—with just the right push in the right place—into the Tipping Point. Ultimately, this offers society hope for positive change and intelligent action where it is needed.

Hayzlett J. Top 3 Traits of a Good Mentor. Entrepreneur. 2017.

According to this article, mentors should have three key traits: generosity, honesty, and discretion.

1. *Generosity.* Good mentors share what they know because they want to improve the organization and "pay it forward." The key for the mentee is to be mindful of the mentor's time. Mentoring takes time and commitment, but not all interactions need be lengthy and involved.
2. *Honesty.* Honest, specific feedback is what the best mentors provide. They will provide the kind of constructive criticism that can be used to build upon as the mentee's career advances and becomes ever more complex.
3. *Discretion.* There absolutely must be trust that confidences will be maintained by the mentor, especially when the mentor is someone within the mentee's organization.

Too many negative outcomes can come from a breach of such confidence. If warranted, a mentee may be best served to find a mentor outside of the organization to avoid this particular issue altogether.

Hudson P. Mentoring as Professional Development: "Growth for Both" Mentor and Mentee. Profession Dev Ed. 2013;39:771-83.

This mixed-methods study surveyed and interviewed experienced mentors. The survey data indicated that mentors evaluate and articulate teaching practices as part of their mentoring, while the interviews described how mentoring acted as professional development. The act of mentoring enhanced communication skills, developed leadership roles (problem-solving and building capacity), and advanced teaching practice knowledge. The study concludes that providing professional development to teachers on mentoring can help to build capacity through explicit mentoring practices but also by reflecting and deconstructing teaching practices for mentors' own teaching advancements.

Humphrey HJ. Mentoring in Academic Medicine. Philadelphia, PA: ACP Press; 2010.

Medical educators and leaders are often involved in mentoring at various points during their careers, and for good reason. Mentorship is a crucial component of success in the healthcare sector, but only if it's done effectively and mindfully.

This book collects insight on mentorship from a variety of experienced medical educators. The various viewpoints and mentoring styles illustrate the fact that mentorship is not—and cannot be—a one-size-fits-all approach. Rather, it needs to be crafted and customized to the mentors and mentees, their career statuses and goals, and the needs of the institution.

Young physicians, for instance, must acquire professional behaviors that take root on a deep, personal level. These behaviors must be nurtured through effective mentors and role models. Mentors of young physicians must seek to understand the new generation of leaders to create a supportive work culture in which people can ask for help—and receive it.

Fostering professionalism in medical students helps establish desirable behaviors and values early in a medical career. This is accomplished through setting an example of honesty and respect and being clear about expectations.

While residents may resist or avoid mentorship due to a perceived lack of time, organizations should strongly encourage mentorship for those entering both academic and clinical positions. Programs designed to recruit mentors and encourage residents to be mentees can lead to more mentorships, paving the way for excellence in future physicians.

Comprehensive programs for faculty in academic medicine are lacking in many institutions. But the body of evidence suggests that mentorship should be prioritized for this group because it can create important relationships and learning opportunities that lead to greater job satisfaction and higher-quality patient care. Therefore, mentorship should be viewed as a vehicle for achieving excellence throughout the organization, not something that simply benefits physicians as individuals.

Faculty programs may consider peer mentoring when experienced faculty are in short supply; this type of mentoring boosts self-confidence in faculty mentors and mentees and provides an opportunity for more personal, candid feedback as well as meaningful professional relationships.

While the traditional model of an experienced teacher and a novice is valuable and perhaps the most widely implemented, other forms of mentoring can be equally beneficial. Mentoring groups and peer-to-peer mentoring can also be empowering and equally educational.

Being supportive of a mentee is perhaps the most significant characteristic of an effective mentor, but other qualities—including being available, respectful, and involved; providing effective and positive feedback; and finding a balance between managing and freedom for the protégé—are equally important.

Sometimes simply doing and being something, rather than teaching it overtly, is a powerful way to pass on both knowledge and morals. This "role model" approach has a profound effect on mentees within the medical field. As such, leaders should be conscious of their behaviors and practice regular self-reflection.

Mentees also must assume responsibility for the success of their own mentorship through realistic expectations, passion, and willingness to accept criticism and responsibility for their actions.

Mentorship offers opportunities in academic medicine that are difficult—if not impossible—to replicate in its absence. The goal of mentorship in medicine ultimately should be to provide better patient care, says Humphrey. Mentorship can provide opportunities for mentees to challenge their own preconceived beliefs, thereby enhancing empathy and tolerance. Telling the truth and speaking up for others, even if initially met with resistance, is an important concept to teach mentees at all levels and one that has the power to transform both medical education and patient care for the better.

Kuhl JS. Investing in Millennials for the Future of Your Organization. Leader to Leader. 2014;71:25-30.

The millennials are the next dominant generation, which means they will soon fill out the ranks of every organization. Companies have struggled to retain top millennial talent due in part to older generations negatively stereotyping millennials as self-centered, immature, or lazy. This article states that organizations need to overcome this acrimony and embrace the upcoming generation if they want to thrive in the coming years.

Because this generation has grown up with technology at their fingertips, they are connected in a way no previous generation has been. Therefore, what looks like nonconformity or laziness to an older coworker—when a millennial requests time off or doesn't want to work a nine-to-five shift—is actually a more integrated approach to work-life balance. Technology extends the workspace beyond the physical location of the office, and this is the first generation to fully embrace that. Millennials tend to have a preference for short, frequent, and electronic communications rather than formal, lengthy, face-to-face meetings. They value results over bureaucracy and flexibility in work hours and communication practices.

All of these things require organizations to adapt if they want to attract and retain millennial talent. Given that the millennial generation will in the not-so-distant future run global business and politics, it is vital for organizations to keep up. That requires redefining expectations around behavior and results to be flexible and accommodating in a way not typically seen in the past. The key idea is to make sure management is open-minded and supportive of the young talent. Leaders should make millennials feel as if they can grow and achieve their full potential within their organization. Managers must continue to sell the opportunity to work for the organization not only because it reinvigorates the young talent but because it gives them the chance to extend your message outward and become part of the recruitment process. Millennials share their experiences across their various social networks in a way no previous generation has, and organizations need to take advantage of that.

Millennials are generally more concerned with the importance of their work than what they are paid to do it, so organizations should connect their work with the company's mission to keep them engaged. Work-life balance must be respected, means to give back to the community should be provided and matched, and personal and professional development programs need to be offered. Development programs should include mentorship, experiential learning, and team-based project work. As with their preferred meeting style, frequent—even real-time—feedback on their performance is key rather than waiting for a typical annual performance review. For those exceptional talents, it is important that there is a challenging career path for them to follow, since millennials typically value results over tenure and see little value in having to "put in time" before demonstrating their skills by taking on difficult projects.

Lewis KR. 5 Mentor Mistakes to Avoid. Fortune. 2014.

The authors of this article present five common mistakes to avoid in mentorship:

1. ***Having a mentor just like you.*** Many people feel they need to find a mentor with a background similar to their own. That is ultimately limiting, however, and not as beneficial as many may assume. Working with someone from a different racial or cultural or gender background presents an opportunity to learn and grow, adding a new perspective to your worldview.

2. ***Asking for general help.*** Be specific and targeted with your goal when engaging with a mentor (or potential mentor). Part of the process of finding a mentor (or mentors) can help identify areas of weakness, which will in turn help you identify the mentors that can help.

3. **Wasting time.** Be prepared and efficient when interacting with your mentor. Set meeting agendas and direct the conversation while following up promptly on anything that comes out of the meeting.

4. **Thinking it's a one-way relationship.** The best mentor-mentee dyads work both ways, and the mentors can often get just as much energy from the interaction as the mentee.

5. **Forcing the relationship.** Often mentorship needs to happen in an organic fashion, either because people are uncomfortable being directly asked to mentor or simply because it doesn't need to be explicitly stated to work. It is likely a mentee will have more than one mentor during their career, including simultaneously, which can reduce the pressure to extract everything they can from any one mentor.

Liu A. It Takes Two: A Guide to Being a Good Mentee. ABA J. 2019.

This article encourages mentees to make their own mentorship opportunities, offering ways to add value back to mentors and find a variety of mentors who have different experience under their belts.

- **Be worth the time and energy.** Mentees should demonstrate more than just great work products—they should show a commitment to the organization. Since mentors are not typically financially compensated for their mentoring, the mentee must make it worth it for them in other ways.

- **Steer the process.** The mentee should initiate contact with a mentor and guide the relationship with regular contact. They should be open and honest and genuinely ready to learn.

- **Develop reciprocity.** Good mentees have something to offer back to the mentor, though what that is will vary by mentor and mentee. Often it can be something seemingly minor, or even something personal.
- **Build a diversified board.** The traditional mentor-mentee dyad is becoming an outmoded idea, so mentees should seek to build a personal "board of directors" who bring diverse skills and experience the mentee can learn. The mentee should consciously look across gender, age, and ethnic boundaries to broaden their perspectives with those of people different from themselves.
- **Your mentors don't have to sit in the corner office.** Anyone has the potential to be a mentor, so a mentee should consider others who may have knowledge or skills that could benefit them.
- **You don't have to be your mentor's "mini-me."** Mentees should want to benefit from each mentor's unique experience, but they must always tailor that knowledge to their own careers and lives.
- **Leverage institutional resources to air your mentoring relationship.** Many institutions have programs that can function as mentoring opportunities, even if they aren't positioned explicitly as mentoring. Many organizations offer some kind of shadowing program, which can be invaluable as mentees begin their careers.
- **Be appreciative.** Mentees should explicitly thank their mentors, either through things like cards or by publicly pointing out their contributions to the mentee's career.
- **Champion other women.** Mentees should actively seek out ways to support women's careers in the people around you—especially if they themselves are a woman.

Liu B. The 4 Types of Mentors You Need in Your Life to Succeed. Inc. 2015.

This article covers four types of mentors and what each has to offer. Each one of these types is necessary for and contributes something unique to a mentee's career, according to the author.

1. **The Coach.** Just like the soccer coach you had as a kid, a coaching mentor is there to help the mentee through tough moments, identify big ideas, and help solve specific problems.
2. **The Connector.** This rare type of mentor excels at helping people network through their own extensive connections. Though rare, these are the types of mentors that you hang on to.
3. **The Cheerleader.** This person is always in your corner, there to cheer for your successes, console you through the hardships, and always support you no matter what.
4. **The Challenger.** This is the realist everyone needs, in order to keep in check the irrational beliefs we all tend to trick ourselves into believing. Though they may burst your bubble, you will appreciate their perspective later, because the Challenger can help set you—or keep you—on the right path.

Llopis G. Mentoring Gone Wrong Can Create Long-Lasting Damage. Forbes. 2012.

"Mentoring gone wrong is common and the damage inflicted could last a life time."

This author relates an example of one type of mentor malpractice through the story of the author and one of his mentors who attempted to shape him in his own image and then tried to subsume the author's successes into his own. The impacts of this kind of mal-practice can be far-ranging, as the author notes, even showing up in the mentee's personal life. Lucky for this particular mentee, he recognized what was happening and did the only thing he really could—pulled back from the mentor in order to reestablish his own identity independent of the mentor.

The article notes that seniority does not automatically qualify someone to be a good mentor. Central to the idea of a good mentor is the mentor's intention to help the mentee improve in and of them-selves and not for any reason that might directly help the mentor. The best mentors know that their best mentees will outgrow them at some point, and that is never a point of contention. On the con-trary, good mentors are rewarded by the knowledge of their mentee's successes—not the successes themselves.

Markman A. The Five Types of Mentors You Need. Fast Company. 2015.

This article covers five types of mentors that should be part of a mentoring team and what each has to offer.

1. *The Coach.* A good coach doesn't solve the mentee's prob-lems for them but listens to what they say and asks ques-tions to lead them to the cause. The coach might suggest strategies for solving problems that can be internalized to guide the mentee past future roadblocks. A good coach can also suggest perspectives on a problem the mentee hasn't thought about, thus broadening their horizons.
2. *The Star.* These are the ones who represent what the men-tee aspires to be. The mentee should get to know them but also observe them—see how they interact and what seems to contribute to their success.

3. **The Connector.** This is the person who knows everyone and can offer to make an introduction. Connectors are an invaluable resource.
4. **The Librarian.** These are the people who know the organization inside and out. Hanging out with them will let the mentee avoid reinventing the wheel or missing out on access to a resource the organization has available.
5. **The Teammate.** This is the person who can walk the fine line between offering a sympathetic ear and helping the mentee move on when negative things happen. Sometimes they don't need a solution—just validation that what they experienced was rough.

The article concludes by saying that the more traditional mentor idea—called "The Advisor"—should not be on the mentorship team. In order to excel, the mentee must learn how to best do their job, not merely copy the success of others.

Mattern J. The Most Valuable Lessons I've Learned from My Mentor. Fast Company. 2015.

The author of this piece relates some advice from her mentor that affects any number of aspects of one's career.

- **Don't name numbers first.** One key to successful negotiation is not to be the first to mention money. The example provided is a job offer, in which it behooves the potential employee to wait for the potential employer to reveal their offer.
- **Make bold moves.** They leave an impression.
- **No one likes a novel-length email.** Everyone is busy. If it can be said in three sentences, leave it there.

- **Ask for what you want.** As the author's mentor said, "Work hard and make them love you."
- **Even your idols are human.** Never be intimidated by reputation or prestige. We are all human.
- **Make meaningful connections.** One way to connect is by sharing personal details, when appropriate. By doing so, you can deepen the connection so that it might last a lifetime.
- **Talk about your pets.** Everyone loves to!

Meister JC, Willyerd K. Mentoring Millennials. Harv Bus Rev. 2010.

This article suggests ways of mentoring that better suit millennials' desires for immediacy and close collaboration with people at all levels of an organization: reverse, group, and anonymous mentoring.

- **Reverse mentoring.** In this form, the millennial would be the mentor to a more senior member of the organization. In teaching the senior (and typically older) member about some specific topic (e.g., social media), the millennial gains insight into and exposure to parts of the organization they may otherwise not work with. In the process, the millennial will organically pick up tips from the mentee that would fit in the more traditionally molded dyad and may potentially gain an accelerated career track, since the mentoring arrangement would likely raise their profile among other senior executives.
- **Group mentoring.** Since mentoring can be resource intensive, this forms an alternative that is less so by having one senior manager or even peer-to-peer groups mentor. This is often set up in the context of a technology platform that

allows for content sharing, scheduling, and messaging. These can even be tailored to provide more real-time feedback by using "microfeedback" (feedback limited to some very small number of characters, like 140). That allows for more rapid feedback, since the responses must be so short.

- *Anonymous mentoring.* Beginning with a psychological and background test, this method matches mentees with mentors who function outside the organization. This would be done via an external contract or service, typically paid for by the company. Interaction is done online, completely anonymously, which can allow for a kind of frankness and honesty that can never be attained in any other traditional dyad arrangement. One added benefit of this setup is that the mentor and mentee don't even have to live on the same side of the planet, let alone the same city or town.

Everyone wants the kind of flexibility millennials are demanding in their work arrangements. Millennials are just the first generation to make those demands heard.

Page SE. The Difference: How the Power of Diversity Creates Better Groups, Firms, Schools, and Societies. Princeton, NJ: Princeton University Press; 2007.

Human problem-solving and reasoning should not be confined to the vacuum of a single person; rather, it is collective thinking with multiple people that often produces excellence. This diversity of minds can be a key factor in breakthroughs and innovations in nearly any field.

Diversity, in this book, deals not necessarily with race, ethnicity, or culture but with variations in how people process and solve problems. While a person's mindset and thinking ability are certainly shaped by one's background, it is each person's cognitive diversity, not their identity diversity, that is the focus of Page's research.

In the workplace, factors such as a high IQ and exceptional intelligence are valuable prerequisites for decision making and leadership. But an exceptional mind, working alone, often cannot match the results of a group of good minds working together. While IQ tests and measures of intelligence have value, they are not necessarily predictors of success. A diverse combination of abilities, mindsets, and thought processes often adds up to more creativity, innovation, and ultimately, more successful outcomes for both people and organizations. This is achieved through the simple fact that the people in any group are different from one another.

Page provides examples of group thinking outperforming individuals, even if the individual is considered an expert. A zoologist and a physicist together uncovered the structure of DNA—without a microscope. Their diverse ways of thinking and backgrounds were the right combination for a groundbreaking discovery that neither one likely would have accomplished alone. But Page does state that group thinking is not always superior to individuals; rather, he presents a balanced overview of how a diverse group can—and often does—achieve solutions more quickly and creatively than a single expert could on their own.

People's thought processes can be likened to tools: One person may have a saw, while the other has a hammer. Separately, they can't do much, but together, they can construct buildings. And so it goes with people's various cognitive tools and their ability to do much more in combination than alone. While there may be tool overlap, and one may have more tools than another, the critical factor is that each person has tools that are used in conjunction with their other abilities, and the tools are used in their own style.

Each person's role also will affect how and why different tools are used. A woman who is both a mother and an executive will use different cognitive abilities and influences when making decisions about her children versus her Monday afternoon staff meeting. These roles can be used to add to the richness of people's perspectives and approaches to discovery and learning.

Page suggests people should "leave their silos" to interact with others who can help each of us find better solutions for problems, especially complex or difficult ones. Differences should not merely be tolerated; rather, diversity should be embraced as an opportunity and possibility for everyone to achieve more in their respective fields.

Prossack A. How to Be a Great Mentee. Forbes. 2018.

This article details seven ways to maximize the benefits of a mentoring relationship for a mentee.

1. ***Take action.*** A mentor is there to help the mentee do their work better. That means the mentee must operationalize the skills learned from the relationship.
2. ***Ask questions.*** Mentees must want to learn, to improve, and to grow. They should drive the conversation with their mentor by asking questions or debating a topic they are passionate about.
3. ***Don't be afraid to disagree.*** A mentee shouldn't feel required to silently accept the words of the mentor. If there is disagreement, it should be discussed, since that conversation can have more value than being compliant.
4. ***Be open to feedback.*** Mentees must be able to accept critical feedback, since that is in part what the mentor is there

to provide for them. Closing down to such input will only limit the positive impact of the relationship.

5. *Be clear on your needs.* Goals give the mentee a focus to make consistent progress and achieve results. They should make sure that those goals are clear with the mentor from the start.

6. *Respect your mentor.* Mentees should show up to meetings prepared and on time and should limit contact to what the mentor expects and is willing to provide.

7. *Be committed.* Being a great mentee means being dedicated to learning and practicing new skills, and that should be a constant, long-term goal.

Rashid B. 3 Reasons All Great Leaders Have Mentors (and Mentees). Forbes. 2017.

This article identifies three significant reasons that many of the greatest leaders have had mentors.

1. *Get pushed out of the comfort zone.* Three particular types of mentors will push mentees out of their comfort zones: "The Challenger" (who asks why the mentee has the comfort zone they do), "The Cheerleader" (who provides enough of a boost to confidence for the mentee to step over the boundaries of their comfort zone), and "The Coach" (who provides the knowledge to overcome the adversity so the mentee can innovate).

2. *Accept and give feedback.* A mentee has essentially requested that the mentor give criticism all the time, so it is crucial that they are (or become) comfortable with accepting it. On the flip side, if a mentor isn't exceptionally skilled at delivering criticism, the act of being a mentor will provide ample opportunity to practice.

3. **Gain a confidant.** Mentorship—especially long-term mentorship—often closely resembles friendship, but in some ways, it needs to be even more than that. The degree of trust required for a truly productive mentoring relationship must be total, communication must be clear, and there should be frequent contact. That means each party has a confidant to share their passion and vent their frustrations, reducing stress for both mentor and mentee.

Saint S, Chopra V. How Doctors Can Be Better Mentors. Harv Bus Rev. 2018.

Physicians have an ethical duty to act in the best interests of their patients, just as mentors have the same duty for their mentees. By practicing mindfulness when approaching either of these interactions, doctors can be better at both.

Both positions—doctor and mentor—involve an asymmetric power balance with the other party. The doctor in both cases has the better part of that power, so it is incumbent upon them to ensure that they focus on the interests and well-being of their patient or mentee. Four guiding principles can help ensure what's best for the mentee.

1. **Be available.** People in healthcare are busy, but taking on a mentee is a responsibility that requires attention. Make any time you can for meetings, even if it's only 15 minutes. While it may be best to meet in person, utilize technology to communicate when unable to meet. During any kind of interaction with your mentee, be mindful and stay present.
2. **Know your role.** The traditional mentor role is the most well known, but you may need to act as a coach, sponsor, or connector for some mentees. Be sure to identify how best

you can help each individual mentee. No matter how you assist your mentee, be mindful and reflective on your role in their careers.

3. ***Try to be objective.*** Mindfulness helps keep you present, but it also requires being nonjudgmental and supportive. The emotional distance required to act in this way also allows you to avoid reacting reflexively if strong emotions emerge during an interaction.

4. ***Put yourself in their shoes.*** Be mindful of the fact that the people you help are important. Actively place yourself in their position in your mind just before interacting with them. It will allow you to be more empathetic and compassionate in your role.

All of this takes time, patience, and perseverance to accomplish. Practice being fully present to start with, then see how that first step unlocks the rest.

Saint S, Chopra V. Thirty Rules for Healthcare Leaders. Ann Arbor, MI: Michigan Publishing, University of Michigan Library; 2019.

While the business world focuses on dollars and capital, the healthcare sector relies upon making a distinctive impact with their resources. For this reason, healthcare leadership is markedly different from business leadership—and should be addressed accordingly.

The rules listed by Drs. Saint and Chopra are geared toward both "assigned leaders" who occupy leadership positions in healthcare and "emergent leaders," or those who have influence regardless of title or position.

It's not simply *how* you lead but *who* you lead that matters. Gathering the right team from the beginning is a way to save time and hassle. It's better to wait for the right candidate than to hire someone quickly who may or may not fit the job. Hiring someone who is less than ideal often adds up to a drain of your time for management, or worse, a difficult process of removal.

Healthcare leaders should have direct discussions with followers about expectations and responsibilities. Each follower should know their role within the organization's mission. Be tight with goals and objectives and hold followers accountable. But be "loose" in terms of letting followers find their own ways to achieve their goals.

Stress is an unavoidable part of healthcare, especially in leadership. Practicing mindfulness regularly can decrease or disable the body's stress response. Remaining calm in a less-than-ideal or even disastrous situation is also a useful strategy to employ but requires practice. Don't become so relaxed, however, that complacency takes hold. Some stress and pressure are helpful and optimize both learning and patient care.

Be on time and end meetings on time—or better yet, early. Bear in mind that the simple act of talking is a barrier to learning, and learning is an integral part of healthcare. Listen more than you talk.

Healthcare leaders should possess a hearty amount of emotional intelligence. In other words, they must have the ability to assess and adjust their own feelings and how they manage them. Emotional intelligence can be practiced and taught, and the more a leader has, the more successful they will be.

Forgive an honest mistake and accept it as part of every human's growth process. But leaders should not forget the mistake itself, lest they risk allowing it to happen again. Let go of blame, resentment, or judgment but remember the incident and the lessons it offers. Expect that no one gets everything right—including you—and practice the art of patience with yourself and your followers.

A healthcare leader's behavior, reactions, social media posts, and words may be scrutinized, misinterpreted, and possibly adopted and emulated by others. As such, it's important to behave in a way that fosters a positive and healthy environment within the healthcare organization. Refrain from jokes and off-the-cuff remarks. Decide what is acceptable behavior for your staff and be a role model for it—and keep followers accountable for adhering to it.

Mentorship is a necessary—not optional—component in successful healthcare organizations. Effective mentors create high-performing employees and successful institutions. But mentors who engage in "malpractice" can be poisonous. Such malpractices include taking credit for a mentee's ideas or work, stalling progress, or simply not taking the time to regularly connect with the mentee and offer opportunities.

Conversely, mentees should remember that they too possess an important responsibility in holding up their end of the bargain: they must meet deadlines, deliver what they promise, and be engaged and eager to learn without requiring hand-holding.

Don't underestimate the value of small things that make the work environment more pleasant and positive. Smile when you see others and be quick to make friends while still maintaining a professional demeanor. Even difficult conversations can be delivered with kindness, respect, and candor. Don't avoid awkward discussions but address them with a positive outcome in mind.

Don't become so wrapped up with your professional life that you forget the personal. Family members and friends provide a necessary sense of purpose and well-being that cannot be duplicated with work.

Perhaps the most important difference between business and healthcare leadership, the authors state, lies in one of the most simple and beautiful behaviors: kindness. Without compassion and love for patients, colleagues, and followers, there is no growth and, ultimately, no true success.

Sandberg J. With Bad Mentors, It's Better to Break Up Than to Make Up. The Wall Street Journal. 2008.

Bad mentoring relationships are not just unhelpful to mentees; they can be downright harmful, according to this article. Emphasizing the need for mentees to have multiple mentors (referring to such as a "polygamous" arrangement), the article uses the language of romantic relationships to frame why getting out of a bad mentoring situation can be just as difficult and painful as leaving a bad personal relationship, while providing some anecdotes of particularly difficult mentorship situations.

Straus S, Sackett D. Mentorship in Academic Medicine. Hoboken, NJ: John Wiley & Sons; 2013.

An evidence-based guide for developing successful mentoring relationships in the context of academic medicine, this book offers cases that take the reader through the evidence for best practices for preventing or correcting problems that arise in a mentoring relationship. In addition, an online resource accompanies the book, providing multimedia resources filled with mentorship tips and strategies. The website also maintains an updated list of departmental and institutional templates for effective mentoring programs.

Tjan AK. What the Best Mentors Do. Harv Bus Rev. 2017.

"The best leaders practice a form of leadership that is less about creating followers and more about creating other leaders," this article begins, then details four key qualities these leader-mentors possess:

1. **Put the relationship before the mentorship.** As noted in other works, one of the fundamental keys to a successful mentorship is the dynamic of the underlying relationship between mentor and mentee. Make the relationship of higher import than going through the motions of mentoring to add it to your CV.

2. **Focus on character rather than competency.** Skills can be acquired in any number of well-established ways, and in mentoring, skill acquisition shouldn't be the primary focus. Mentors should focus instead on bringing out and shaping the character of the mentee, emphasizing "values, self-awareness, empathy, and [a] capacity for respect."

3. **Shout loudly with your optimism and keep quiet with your cynicism.** "Consider why an idea might work, before you consider why it might not." In doing so, you will be supporting and encouraging your mentee in their pursuits.

4. **Be more loyal to your mentee than you are to your company.** Mentors should identify their mentees' passion— their calling. Don't simply try to find those qualities that best serve the organization, but help the mentee toward their true potential.

Tobin M. Mentoring: Seven Roles and Some Specifics. Am J Respir Crit Care Med. 2004.

This article synthesizes many sources to describe the seven roles mentors can fill: Teacher, Sponsor, Advisor, Agent, Role Model, Coach, and Confidante.

1. **Teachers** impart specific knowledge to the mentee, such as reading efficiently, reasoning from first principles, or writing scientific manuscripts. Knowing that education is not

so much about facts as it is about character development, the Teacher focuses on shaping the "moral backbone" of the mentee.

2. **Sponsors** connect new researchers to the social network of their peers, providing invaluable advice on who to seek out for input and who to avoid. The Sponsor also helps shape the values and customs of science into rising mentees.

3. **Advisors** offer the mentee an opportunity to talk about issues they may be facing, listening and helping the mentee become ever more self-reliant. Often, for the mentor, this process is one of listening as the mentee works out their own solutions. Providing thoughtful advice when requested is invaluable, though. This type of mentoring should not be confused with faculty advising, something many students are accustomed to. Mentor-mentee dyads are typically much more personal than faculty advisor-student relationships.

4. **Agents** should always be ready to help a mentee clear obstacles in their path, though the mentee needs to make a "convincing attempt" to do this on their own first. But the mentee should know that if they try and fail, the mentor will clear the way.

5. **Role Models** demonstrate the values their mentees should emulate. From professional priorities to making work enjoyable, the mentee should be able to see the qualities they admire in their mentor and strive to make them part of their own approach to work and science.

6. **Coaches** motivate the mentee to success, knowing when to push and when to wait for the mentee to arrive at a point on their own. The mentor sets high standards for the mentee to strive for and helps them reach for and

achieve those goals. Expectations are high but always attainable.

7. **Confidantes** are the ones the mentee can confide in, knowing that whatever is said will unequivocally remain confidential. More than any other, that is a relationship built on trust, which is earned through constancy, reliability, integrity, and congruity.

All mentors share some qualities. Failure is a part of growth, and any mentor must help their mentee learn to work through failures to find the next success. Mentors will instill several key steps to success in their mentees, including persistence, focus, time management, and handling credit.

The author concludes with some advice for mentees as well, starting with things to look for when choosing a mentor. A mentor should be chosen for their enthusiasm in their research topic, for having the time to take on a (or another) mentee, for the quality of their leadership abilities, and for their commitment, common sense, competence, responsibility, and conscience. It is possible for mentors to be bad for the mentee, such as when they are selfish with their time or hoard the successes of the mentee as their own. When mentors envy the attention the mentee may get, that can cause problems in the dynamic of the relationship. A mentor who too much tries to shape the mentee in their own image or is too overprotective can also harm the potential of the mentee and their own individual trajectory in their career.

At times, it can be challenging for mentees to find a suitable match where they are, so it is important for some mentees to recognize that they can find influence and resources in many forms, including books, as some very influential people from history have done.

Finally, the article points out that mentoring is not a one-way activity. Both parties ultimately benefit from a fruitful mentor-mentee dyad.

Ury W. The Power of a Positive No: How to Say No and Still Get to Yes. New York, NY: Bantam Books; 2007.

Saying "no" is a necessary component of personal and professional interactions. While most people know how to do this, many don't do it in a way that is honest, respectful, and considerate of the recipient. The wrong kind of "No" can damage—or end—the best relationships.

This risk can be avoided, however, by delivering a No with specific intentions and strategies.

Ury suggests, first, to deliver your No with a "Yes." This means focusing inward on one's core interests without projecting anything onto the other person. Avoid rejection or attacking of the other's ideas. This can ward off feelings of fear, anger, or defensiveness. It does not, however, guarantee that the other person will be on board with your response.

At this point, you may have to further protect and advance your own interests and priorities. Be prepared for pushback and develop a backup plan to utilize if the other person does not accept or cooperate. This "Plan B" is not a punishment or a way to act out anger or frustration. Rather, it's a means of providing resolve and determination during a negotiation without fear or anxiety over the other person's reaction.

When delivering a No, your goal is to get the other person to accept it. Start with a positive statement that affirms that you have listened to their viewpoint. Acknowledge their side and let them have their say. Ask clarifying questions when needed. Affirm the person's value but stay firm on your stance with the issue. Be respectful as you deliver your No.

Explaining the reasons behind your No is an integral part of getting the other person to accept it. Use "I" statements that express your own interests or needs and "we" statements that promote shared interests. Avoid "you" statements that put the other person on defense. Don't judge the other person or offer unsolicited advice on what they "should" do. Avoid "always" and "never." Stick to the facts and address the issue and/or behavior, not the person. If a situation is uncomfortable or inappropriate, however, a firm "no" without explanation may be warranted.

The purpose of your No is to set boundaries on what is important to you. Be assertive, not aggressive. A No is best delivered clearly and calmly and with honesty and respect. This can be done without worry over the other person's reaction, something over which you have no control. The purpose of your No is to defend yourself without attacking the other party.

Tell the other person what you *will* do rather than what you *won't*. It gives them the opportunity to provide their own No, which can diffuse discomfort and ill feelings on their part. Propose a third option that offers an agreeable compromise. When you give your No, make a constructive request that clarifies the action or result you *want*, not what you *don't* want. Be sure the request is feasible and delivered with respect and positive intention.

Feelings of guilt and fear over delivering your No may make you prone to wavering. Show respect and empathy for the other person, but don't allow these things to weaken your No. Control your own reaction and pause before speaking. Acknowledge how they feel, but don't give in to their request. A lack of emotional reaction on your part can help to soften anxiety or anger in the other person.

If the other person won't accept your No, you do not respond by waging a war or with submission. Instead, you underscore your No in a positive fashion. Keep repeating it and offer your Plan B if necessary. In repeating and underscoring your No, you form a boundary that protects your stance without yielding or attacking.

Search for an agreement that fulfills your needs and addresses the other person's needs as well, without compromising on the things you have resolved not to do. If you come to an agreement, consider other key players who also need to get on board with it.

Look for ways to nourish your relationship with people to whom you must say No. Ury's approach aims to empower people to stand up for what they believe in while finding constructive solutions that benefit all sides of the discussion.

Valerio AM, Sawyer K. The Men Who Mentor Women. Harv Bus Rev. 2016.

On the basis of a rigorous qualitative analysis of 75 interviews with managers at various levels of organizations, this article articulates four themes that emerged that were associated with gender-inclusive leadership.

1. *Using their authority to change workplace culture.* In both obvious and more subtle ways, men can use their positions to elevate the visibility and impact women can have in a culture that has traditionally not accepted them. This often requires men to directly challenge their male colleagues operating under a double standard or outmoded models of behavior toward women.
2. *Thinking of gender inclusiveness as part of effective talent management.* Under any circumstance in which women are excluded, organizations have effectively cut

their potential talent pool in half. Recruiting, identifying, and planning for future advancement of women is another part of talent management.

3. **Providing gender-aware mentoring and coaching.** Putting women in positions where they can excel, succeed, and be visible while doing it is one direct impact senior males can have on women through mentoring and coaching. Just being a part of projects can increase visibility through higher ranks of an organization, as the female mentee's name becomes familiar to senior leadership—even if they haven't met personally yet. Being mentored and coached not only increases earnings and career satisfaction; it also brings greater self-confidence.

4. **Practicing other-focused leadership, not self-focused leadership.** For cross-gender mentorship to succeed, mentors must be allies—that is, they must be actively striving to end gender prejudice in both their personal and professional lives. Developing leadership in others requires the mentor to step back from their interest in their own power in order for the mentee to be seen on their own merits. In other words, the mentor must have a strong altruistic streak, with an interest in developing for the organization or the field, and not just their own careers.

Vaughn V, Saint S, Chopra V. Mentee Missteps: Tales from the Academic Trenches. JAMA. 2017;317:475–6.

This piece details two different groups of three types of mentees and the mistakes they typically make. It has advice for both mentors and mentees, as these mistakes are landmines waiting to be stepped on and damage a mentoring relationship unless carefully avoided!

- The Conflict Averse
  1. *The Overcommitter.* The "yes person"—the one who can't say "no." Overcommitters often end up disillusioned and/or burned out.
  2. *The Ghost.* Avoiding the problems confronting them, Ghosts are merely delaying the inevitable, and their actions often doom the mentoring relationship as mistrust accumulates.
  3. *The Doormat.* Rarely noticed but often used. They spend their time doing tasks that require extensive time and effort but offer little reward or advancement.
- The Confidence Lacking
  1. *The Vampire.* Typified by countless emails, text messages, phone calls, and meeting requests, these mentees are paralyzed by decision making and rely on mentors for validation.
  2. *The Lone Wolf.* Although these may appear stubborn or even confident, internally they fear asking for help lest they appear weak or foolish, yet their downfall often comes from an avoidable, yet embarrassing, event.
  3. *The Backstabber.* Their inability to accept culpability eventually leads Backstabbers to sacrifice others when errors occur, shunning blame rather than accepting responsibility.

Waljee JF, Chopra V, Saint S. Mentoring Millennials. JAMA. 2018;319:1547-8.

The authors discuss ways to mentor millennials with specific scenarios that often incite frustration or confusion on both sides of the relationship. It explains the "why" of common millennial behavior that may be foreign to older generations—opening the door to productive collaboration by eliminating stereotypes—through extracting three themes from some common, frustrating scenarios.

1. *As needed vs. scheduled engagement.* Millennials are used to engagement that facilitates quick decision making and expands collaboration networks. For that expectation to be met, accessibility, fast responses, rapid turnaround, and frequent short meetings must be entertained.
2. *Flat vs. pyramidal infrastructure.* Millennials embrace collaboration and cognitive diversity more readily than prior generations. This positions them well for team science, multidisciplinary care, and collective leadership, but flattening social and hierarchical gaps may also lead to conflict with older generations.
3. *Purpose vs. process.* For millennials, purpose is paramount. Millennials often derive greater satisfaction from results and implementation. The established process is not as important.

Zachary LJ. Creating a Mentoring Culture: The Organization's Guide. 1st ed. San Francisco, CA: Jossey-Bass; 2005.

Organizations that implement and prioritize mentorship reap its numerous benefits. Higher morale, job satisfaction, and employee retention; more effective leaders; and enhanced learning for employees at all levels are just some of the ways mentorship can strengthen an institution and the people in it, says Zachary. This book provides background on the need for mentoring, its inherent value, and how organizations can create a mentoring culture, which embeds mentorship into an organization's structure, allowing it to reach its fullest potential.

Change is constant and inevitable, but a mentorship culture creates a means by which growth and success can be achieved within these variables. But the human resources within the organization and the specific components of mentoring must be aligned in critical areas of values, vision, decision making, and strategy. Once a mentoring goal has been set, these components can then be shared at all levels of the organization, making mentorship both meaningful and a conduit to success for individuals and the whole.

Once a mentorship program has been established, utilizing effective communication is necessary to garner interest and enthusiasm throughout the institution. The program must have identified value and visible support from senior management. Role modeling from leaders as well as financial incentives and recognition add both value and visibility.

But interest in mentorship must come organically; that is, employees should have a desire for mentorship because of a motivation to succeed. Leaders should be enthusiastic about mentoring and should take opportunities to discuss it with coworkers. The success of both mentors and mentees should be widely shared and celebrated. These practices must be continual, giving mentorship momentum and feeding ongoing demand. Leaders should continue to participate in and support mentorship, which will lend it credibility.

The author explains that organizations may shy away from valuable mentorship opportunities because they are locked into a notion that mentorship follows only a traditional model of an older, experienced teacher and inexperienced, younger protégé. In fact, accepting various and innovative mentorship models is necessary to supporting a mentorship culture that is inclusive and innovative. For instance, peer, group, team, and reverse mentoring all have their purposes and advantages that promote quality mentorship opportunities.

Creating a mentorship culture requires some preparation and commitment in the form of education and training. Though these two terms are well known and often used interchangeably, they are different—and equally necessary—for an organization that is striving to provide positive mentorship experiences. Education and training should meet the needs of various learning styles whenever possible, and factors such as recruiting a qualified facilitator, a proper setting, and the readiness of employees must be considered before moving forward. If education and training are approached with enthusiasm and discipline, the learners acquire a powerful opportunity for increased confidence, continuous learning, and a greater concept of self-worth.

Even the best-laid mentorship plans result in challenges and roadblocks at times. For this reason, any organization that strives to implement effective mentorship must have processes in place to recover from such setbacks. Of course, the best safety net is good preparation and planning that helps to minimize problems in the first place. Proper education and training, clear expectations, tools and models for the mentor and mentee, and identifying the root cause of the issue are all necessary pieces of the proactive safety net approach.

While implementing a mentorship culture takes time and resources, its benefits are well worth the effort. Mentorship goes beyond improvements for today's workforce: when implemented fully and enthusiastically, mentorship creates a continuous ripple effect that extends to individuals and organizations well into the future.

REFERENCES (BY CHAPTER)

CHAPTER 1: THREE STEPS TO GETTING STARTED AS A MENTOR

1. Chopra V, Saint S. 6 Things Every Mentor Should Do. Harv Bus Rev. 2017.
2. Clark D. Your Career Needs Many Mentors, Not Just One. Harv Bus Rev. 2017.
3. Cole B. A Visit with Historian David McCullough, the 2003 Jefferson Lecturer. NEH. 2003;24:4-5.
4. Hayzlett J. Top 3 Traits of a Good Mentor. Entrepreneur. 2017.
5. Page SE. The Difference: How the Power of Diversity Creates Better Groups, Firms, Schools, and Societies. Princeton: Princeton University Press; 2007.
6. Tjan AK. What the Best Mentors Do. Harv Bus Rev. 2017.

CHAPTER 2: KNOW YOUR ROLE

1. Chopra V, Arora VM, Saint S. Will You Be My Mentor? Four Archetypes to Help Mentees Succeed in Academic Medicine. JAMA Intern Med. 2018;178:175-6.

2. Gladwell M. The Tipping Point: How Little Things Can Make a Big Difference. Boston, MA: Little, Brown; 2006.

3. Liu B. The 4 Types of Mentors You Need in Your Life to Succeed. Inc. 2015.

4. Markman A. The Five Types of Mentors You Need. Fast Company. 2015.

5. Tobin MJ. Mentoring: Seven Roles and Some Specifics. Am J Respir Crit Care Med. 2004;170:114-7.

CHAPTER 3: SIX RULES FOR MINDFUL MENTORING

1. Altman I. The Dos and Don'ts of Mentoring. Forbes. 2017.

2. Blackman A. Misguided Guidance: 12 Mistakes Mentors Should Avoid. Modern Workforce: Everwise. 2014.

3. Cho CS, Ramanan RA, Feldman MD. Defining the Ideal Qualities of Mentorship: A Qualitative Analysis of the Characteristics of Outstanding Mentors. Am J Med. 2011;124:453-8.

4. Chopra V, Edelson DP, Saint S. Mentorship Malpractice. JAMA. 2016;315:1453-4.

5. Saint S, Chopra V. How Doctors Can Be Better Mentors. Harv Bus Rev. 2018.

CHAPTER 4: THE MENTEE'S QUICK-START GUIDE

1. Gallo A. Demystifying Mentoring. Harv Bus Rev. 2011.

2. Liu A. It Takes Two: A Guide to Being a Good Mentee. ABA J. 2019.

3. Rashid B. 3 Reasons All Great Leaders Have Mentors (and Mentees). Forbes. 2017.

CHAPTER 5: NINE THINGS STANDOUT MENTEES DO

1. Chopra V, Dixon-Woods M, Saint S. The Four Golden Rules of Effective Menteeship. BMJ Careers. 2016.
2. Lewis KR. 5 Mentor Mistakes to Avoid. Fortune. 2014.
3. Mattern J. The Most Valuable Lessons I've Learned from My Mentor. Fast Company. 2015.
4. Saint S, Chopra V. Thirty Rules for Healthcare Leaders. Ann Arbor, MI: Michigan Publishing, University of Michigan Library; 2019.
5. Saint S, Chopra V. Leadership & Professional Development: Know Your TLR. J Hosp Med. 2019;14:189.

CHAPTER 6: BEWARE THE MENTEE LANDMINES

1. Chopra V, Edelson DP, Saint S. Mentorship Malpractice. JAMA. 2016;315:1453-4.
2. Hudson P. Mentoring as Professional Development: "Growth for Both" Mentor and Mentee. Profession Dev Ed. 2013;39:771-83.
3. Prossack A. How to Be a Great Mentee. Forbes. 2018.
4. Ury W. The Power of a Positive No: How to Say No and Still Get to Yes. New York, NY: Bantam Books; 2007.
5. Vaughn V, Saint S, Chopra V. Mentee Missteps: Tales from the Academic Trenches. JAMA. 2017;317:475-6.

CHAPTER 7: ENDING RELATIONSHIPS WITH MENTORS

1. Byerley JS. Mentoring in the Era of #MeToo. JAMA. 2018; 319:1199-200.
2. Chopra V, Edelson DP, Saint S. Mentorship Malpractice. JAMA. 2016;315:1453-4.

3. Llopis G. Mentoring Gone Wrong Can Create Long-Lasting Damage. Forbes. 2012.
4. Sandberg J. With Bad Mentors, It's Better to Break Up Than to Make Up. The Wall Street Journal. 2008.

CHAPTER 8: MENTORING ACROSS GENERATIONS

1. Kuhl JS. Investing in Millennials for the Future of Your Organization. Leader to Leader. 2014;71:25-30.
2. Meister JC, Willyerd K. Mentoring Millennials. Harv Bus Rev. 2010.
3. Waljee JF, Chopra V, Saint S. Mentoring Millennials. JAMA. 2018;319:1547-8.

CHAPTER 9: MENTORING ACROSS DIVERSITY WITH A FOCUS ON WOMEN

1. Banaji MR, Greenwald AG. Blindspot: Hidden Biases of Good People. 1st ed. New York: Delacorte Press; 2013.
2. Byerley JS. Mentoring in the Era of #MeToo. JAMA. 2018; 319:1199-200.
3. Choo EK, van Dis J, Kass D. Time's Up for Medicine? Only Time Will Tell. N Engl J Med. 2018;379:1592-3.
4. DeCastro R, Sambuco D, Ubel PA, Stewart A, Jagsi R. Mentor Networks in Academic Medicine: Moving beyond a Dyadic Conception of Mentoring for Junior Faculty Researchers. Acad Med. 2013;88.
5. Farnell R. Mentor People Who Aren't Like You. Harv Bus Rev. 2017.
6. Valerio AM, Sawyer K. The Men Who Mentor Women. Harv Bus Rev. 2016.

7. Verghese A. Resident Redux. Ann Intern Med. 2004;140:1034-6.

8. Moniz M, Saint S. Leadership & Professional Development: Be the Change You Want to See. J Hosp Med. 2019;4;254.

CHAPTER 10: LOOKING BACK WHILE TRAVELING FORWARD

1. Byars-Winston A, Womack VY, Butz AR, et al. Pilot Study of an Intervention to Increase Cultural Awareness in Research Mentoring: Implications for Diversifying the Scientific Workforce. J Clin Transl Sci. 2018;2:86-94.

2. Rabinowitz LG. Recognizing Blind Spots—a Remedy for Gender Bias in Medicine? N Engl J Med. 2018;378:2253-5.

3. Schäfer M, Pander T, Pinilla S, Fischer MR, von der Borch P, Dimitriadis K. The Munich-Evaluation-of-Mentoring-Questionnaire (MEMeQ)—a Novel Instrument for Evaluating Protégés' Satisfaction with Mentoring Relationships in Medical Education. BMC Med Educ. 2015;15:201.

4. Sheridan LMM, Murdock NH, Harder E. Assessing Mentoring Culture: Faculty and Staff Perceptions, Gaps, and Strengths. Can J High Educ. 2015;45:423-39.

ABOUT THE AUTHORS

Dr. Vineet Chopra is Chief of the Division of Hospital Medicine, Associate Professor of Internal Medicine at the University of Michigan, and a Research Scientist at the VA Ann Arbor Healthcare System. Dr. Chopra's research focuses on improving the safety of hospitalized patients through the prevention of hospital-acquired complications. He is the recipient of numerous teaching and research awards including the 2016 Kaiser Permanente Award for Clinical Teaching and has published over 200 peer-reviewed articles in major medical journals. He has also written numerous articles in the Harvard Business Review, JAMA, and the British Medical Journal on mentorship.

Dr. Valerie M. Vaughn is an Assistant Professor of Medicine in the Division of Hospital Medicine at the University of Michigan, and a Research Scientist at the VA Ann Arbor Healthcare System. Her main research interests include antibiotic stewardship—how to optimize the appropriate use of antibiotics for common infections—and why some hospitals are better than others at improving quality. She has first-authored a paper in JAMA on mistakes that mentees make and has spoken at various national venues on mentoring.

Dr. Sanjay Saint is the Chief of Medicine at the VA Ann Arbor Healthcare System and the George Dock Professor of Internal Medicine at the University of Michigan. His research focuses on patient safety, leadership, and medical decision-making. He has authored over 350 peer-reviewed papers in major medical journals including nearly 100 in the New England Journal of Medicine or JAMA. He has also written for the Wall Street Journal, Harvard Business Review, and other major news outlets and has published numerous books. He has written several articles in the Harvard Business Review, JAMA, and the British Medical Journal on mentorship. He received the Mark Wolcott Award from the Department of Veterans Affairs as the National VA Physician of the Year in 2016, and a major mentorship award from the University of Michigan Health System in 2018.

ABOUT THE ARTIST

Danny Suárez is a fourth year student in the Stamps School of Art and Design at the University of Michigan. Their focus is in illustration as well as sequential art and stop motion animation.

More of Danny's work can be found online at suarez.myportfolio .com.